Frugal

Living

Learn Proven Strategies to Start Saving Money

(Learn How to Cut Everyday Expenses in Half and Live Within Your Means)

Paul Richardson

Published By **Cathy Nedrow**

Paul Richardson

*Frugal Living: Learn Proven Strategies to Start
Saving Money (Learn How to Cut Everyday
Expenses in Half and Live Within Your Means)*

ISBN   978-1-7386412-3-9

Legal & Disclaimer

Table Of Contents

Chapter 1: Frugality

Frugality is the exercising of being aware about one's spending and making conscious alternatives to shop cash. It is a manner of lifestyles choice that includes being intentional with how one spends their coins and property. This can encompass reducing lower back on useless costs, locating techniques to keep cash on essential costs, and being aware of 1's everyday intake.

In modern-day economic machine, many humans are dealing with economic uncertainty and instability due to factors which includes interest loss, developing expenses of residing, and stagnant wages. Frugal dwelling may be an powerful way to decorate one's monetary nicely-being in these tough instances.

By reducing prices and developing financial savings, humans can beautify their monetary safety and decrease their dependence on debt. This can provide a protection net for sudden costs and assist human beings collect their economic dreams, together with saving for retirement or paying off student loans.

Frugal dwelling additionally may be useful for the environment. By reducing intake and waste, humans can make contributions to a more sustainable destiny. This can include practices which encompass decreasing power consumption with the aid of way of the use of power-inexperienced domestic system, slicing lower returned on meat intake, and searching for second-hand devices.

However, it's far essential to note that frugal residing isn't always about being cheap or living in poverty. Rather, it's miles about making conscious choices approximately spending and consumption to improve one's financial nicely-being and make contributions to a greater sustainable future.

In order to acquire fulfillment with frugal dwelling, you may begin with the beneficial resource of placing economic goals, monitoring your prices, and developing a budget, greater mild can be shed on all this as you read further on this e-book, It's furthermore important to be realistic and bendy along with your spending and financial financial savings plans, as unexpected prices can rise up.Find a balance among frugality and taking part in existence.

There's no want to reduce out all amusing and satisfaction, but as an possibility try and find out strategies to revel in them in a price range-super way.

Frugality may be a beneficial device for humans to decorate their economic well-being and make a contribution to a greater sustainable destiny in current-day monetary system. It's a way of existence desire that calls for intentionality, balance, and flexibility.

How to make a finances and keep on with it

Creating a price range and sticking to it is able to be an powerful way to manipulate your finances and accumulate your economic goals. Here are some steps you may take to create a charge range and make it be just right for you:

Track your fees: Before you may create a budget, you need to understand in which your coins goes. Keep song of all of your charges for at the least a month to get an concept of your spending patterns.

Set monetary desires: Decide what you need to accumulate together with your charge range. Whether it is saving for a down charge on a house, paying off debt, or constructing an emergency fund, having specific goals will assist you live inspired.

Create a price range: Based in your prices and desires, create a rate range that allocates your cash in a manner that makes experience for you. Be certain to include ordinary prices (like rent and utilities) and variable fees (like groceries and leisure).

Stick to the rate range: Once you have a charge variety in place, preserve on with it as closely as feasible. Be aware about your spending and make modifications as crucial.

Review and modify your charge range often: Your price range want to be a living file which you assessment and regulate often. This will help you live at the proper tune and make changes as your profits or prices exchange.

Use budgeting apps or tools: There are many apps and tools to be had that allow you to create and stick with a price range. These device will can help you tune your prices, create a fee range, and live on top of your rate variety.

Be bendy: Sometimes unexpected expenses rise up, so it's far critical to be bendy collectively collectively with your finances. If something comes up, adjust your price variety consequently and do no longer beat yourself up for overspending.

Reward yourself: Setting and sticking to a rate range may be difficult, so it's far important to reward your self even as you reach your monetary goals.

Creating a price range and sticking to it calls for area, but with time and practice, it may end up a dependancy to help you reap your financial desires. Remember, budgeting is a journey, no longer a holiday spot.

Examples of budgeting apps/gadget

These are few examples of budgeting apps/gadget a good way to assist you to create and hold on with a price variety.

Mint: Mint is a famous budgeting app that lets in you to attach all your economic group debts, credit rating score gambling cards, and investments in one location. It furthermore affords an in depth breakdown of your spending, enables you create a fee range, and signals you even as you are drawing close your charge variety limits.

You Need a Budget (YNAB): YNAB is a budgeting app that makes a speciality of supporting you "live on ultimate month's earnings." It facilitates you create a rate variety based totally definitely on your profits and costs, and offers tools to help you stay with it.

PocketGuard: PocketGuard is an app that allows you create a fee variety and track your spending. It furthermore provides customized economic monetary financial savings suggestions primarily based for your spending conduct.

Wally: Wally is a budgeting app that lets in you track your charges and income. It allows you to take pix of receipts and mechanically categorize your spending.

Spendee: Spendee is a budgeting app that enables you track your prices, create budgets, and set economic savings goals. It moreover permits you to percent your budgets and costs with friends and own family.

Expensify: Expensify is a budgeting app that allows you song fees, manage company costs, and create opinions. It also gives a receipt scanning feature that might routinely import and categorize your expenses.

EveryDollar: EveryDollar is a budgeting app that lets in you create a 0-based totally actually price range, due to this you allocate every greenback of your profits to particular fees.

Goodbudget: Goodbudget is a budgeting app that uses the envelope budgeting technique, which helps you visualize and song your spending in particular lessons.

Choose the most effective that exquisite fits your wishes and opportunities for the first-class cease end result.

Understanding your spending conduct

Understanding your spending behavior is an vital step in growing a finances and handling your finances. Here are a few methods to recognize your spending conduct:

Track your prices: Keep music of all your expenses for at the least a month. This will give you a easy photograph of in which your cash is going and wherein you can make adjustments.

Categorize your costs: Once you have got a listing of all your costs, categorize them into categories together with housing, transportation, groceries, enjoyment, and so on. This will assist you find out styles and areas wherein you'll be overspending.

Chapter 2: Grocery Shopping On A Budget

Meal planning and grocery lists

Meal making plans is a technique of organizing and making plans the meals you could consume for a positive time frame, typically every week. It entails identifying what food you will make, and then growing a grocery list primarily based surely on the components you need for those food. By planning your food in advance, you may avoid impulse buys and overspending on useless gadgets at the grocery store. This will permit you to persist with your fee variety and keep coins on groceries.

When growing your grocery list, it's miles crucial to be particular about the objects you need, and to take into account how an entire lot of each object you may need. This will help you keep away from overbuying and dropping food. Consider checking your pantry and fridge for objects you've got already have been given on hand and ensure you do not purchase them once more.

Shopping at good buy stores, shopping for in bulk, and looking for sales and coupons moreover will let you store cash on groceries. Many bargain shops provide decrease expenses on a big style of products, and seeking out in bulk can save cash on items like rice, beans, and pasta. Sales and coupons can prevent coins on unique devices.

Finally, cooking at home and retaining off consuming out additionally allow you to hold cash on food charges. Eating out is frequently greater expensive than cooking at home, and it may upload up speedy in case you're no longer careful. By cooking at domestic, you could manipulate the elements and element sizes, with the intention to will let you hold money on food costs ultimately.

How to devise food for the week

Planning meals for the week can be finished in a few easy steps:

Assess a while desk: Look at your time table for the week and don't forget any busy days or sports activities that can have an impact on meal planning.

Make a listing of meals: Make a list of meals you need to devour for the week. Consider variety and nutrition. You can use a number of your circle of relatives's favored food, or try new recipes you would love to try.

Create a grocery listing: Based at the food you've got were given planned, create a grocery list of the materials you want. Be amazing to check your pantry and fridge for devices you have already got available to keep away from overbuying.

Prepare and/or prepare dinner in advance: If viable, put together a few food or components earlier. This have to embody prepping greens, marinating meats, or cooking grains in advance of time.

Plan for leftovers: Plan for leftovers with the resource of creating a hint more of advantageous food so you should have them for lunch or dinner day after today.

Keep it flexible: Life takes place, keep in thoughts that your plans might also change, so it's far an outstanding concept to have a few clean, pass-to food available that you could make speedy if desired.

By following those steps, you could have a plan for your food, save cash, and time. Meal planning additionally let you are making more healthy food choices, reduce meals waste and make cooking a lot less annoying.

Strategies for saving coins on groceries.

Make a grocery listing and live with it: Creating a grocery listing and sticking to it permit you to keep away from impulse buys and overspending on needless devices.

Compare fees: Compare expenses amongst tremendous shops and search for income, discounts, and coupons. You also can take a look at fees of various producers of products.

Buy in bulk: Buying in bulk can store coins on objects like rice, beans, and pasta.

Cook at home: Cooking at home is often much less pricey than consuming out, and it allows you to govern the components and element sizes.

Plan food: Planning food earlier let you make the most of the additives you purchase and reduce food waste.

Shop at bargain shops: Shopping at reduce fee shops can prevent coins on a huge shape of products.

Grow your private food: If you have got the distance and time, undergo in mind growing your very own cease give up result and greens. It can save you pretty a few coins ultimately.

Buy frozen or canned: Frozen or canned forestall cease result and vegetables may be a price range-exceptional alternative and might final longer than clean produce.

Buy save brand: Many save-brand products are simply as pinnacle as call-brand products, however at a lower rate.

Use cashback apps or loyalty applications: Many shops and supermarkets offer cashback or loyalty programs which could prevent coins on groceries through the years.

By imposing the ones techniques, you can maintain cash on groceries at the same time as nonetheless getting the objects you want.

How to shop for offers and discounts

Check flyers and circulars: Many supermarkets and retailers supply out weekly flyers and circulars that market it income and reductions. Be first-rate to test the ones for deals on the objects you need.

Look for coupons: Coupons may be determined in newspapers, magazines, and on-line. Look for coupons on products you often buy or are planning to shop for.

Sign up for shop loyalty programs: Many supermarkets and shops offer loyalty applications that supply people get right of access to to tremendous offers and discounts.

Shop online: Many stores provide on-line gives, reductions and unfastened shipping.

Take advantage of clearance profits: Many stores mark down gadgets which is probably about to run out or that they need to get rid of. These items can be placed at a lower rate, however make sure to test the expiry date earlier than shopping for.

Shop in the direction of off-top hours: Many supermarkets and stores provide discounts on first-class devices for the duration of off-height hours, which incorporates late at night time or early in the morning.

You can keep coins on the devices you need even as sticking to your budget. Remember to normally do not forget of the expiration dates and make certain you may use the gadgets earlier than they expire.

Examples of cashback apps

There are many cashback apps available, however a few well-known examples include:

Ibotta: This app allows clients to earn cash lower returned on their grocery purchases with the aid of manner of uploading receipts or linking their loyalty card.

Checkout 51: This app gives coins over again on a wonderful style of products, which consist of groceries, personal care items, and own family items.

Rakuten: This app allows clients to earn cash again when they shop online at over 2,500 stores.

Dosh: This app offers coins lower back at the equal time as customers shop in-save and on-line at lots of retailers, together with Walmart and Target.

Honey: This browser extension automatically applies coupons and searches for the high-quality offers on the identical time as you shop on line.

Shopkick: This app rewards clients for traveling stores and scanning merchandise with their cellphone. Rewards can be redeemed for gift playing cards, discounts, or cashback.

Swagbucks: This internet website and app rewards users for taking surveys, watching films, and buying on-line. Rewards may be redeemed for cashback or present playing cards.

These are only some examples of cashback apps that allow you to keep cash while you keep. Each app has a one-of-a-type desire of stores and merchandise, so it could be worth trying some to appearance which one works excellent for you.

Avoiding impulse buys

Make a grocery list: Before going to the shop, make a list of the items you want and hold on with it. This assist you to avoid searching for pointless gadgets.

Shop with a plan: Have a plan of what to buy in advance than you go to the shop, and hold on with it. This will help you avoid shopping for gadgets on impulse.

Avoid buying when you're hungry: Shopping while you are hungry must make you much more likely to buy gadgets on impulse.

Avoid impulse-purchase aisles: Many shops location impulse-purchase devices which includes sweet and toys near the checkout. Try to avoid those aisles or walk via them quick.

Use cash: Paying with coins will can help you hold song of your spending and avoid overspending on impulse buys.

Avoid looking for gadgets you don't want: Be aware of the matters you have got already have been given at domestic and avoid looking for duplicate gadgets.

Take a damage: If you are not sure if you want an object, take a ruin and don't forget it earlier than growing a final preference.

Wait for a sale: If you aren't sure in case you want an object, sit up for it to move on sale earlier than looking for it.

Chapter 3: Saving Money On Transportation

How to pick out the great mode of transportation on your desires

When deciding on the amazing mode of transportation for your desires, do not forget the subsequent elements:

Distance: For shorter distances, on foot or cycling may be the most price-powerful and environmentally best possibility. For longer distances, public transportation or carpooling may be extra realistic.

Frequency of use: If you will be the usage of the transportation regularly, it may be really really worth making an investment in a monthly pass for public transportation or carpooling.

Cost: Compare the rate of various transportation options, collectively with the fee of gas, parking, and protection for a automobile, similarly to any costs or fares for public transportation or enjoy-sharing offerings.

Speed and luxury: Consider how long it will take to get for your vacation spot and whether or not or not the transportation preference is on hand in your time table and desires.

Environmental impact: Consider the environmental effect of various transportation options and pick one which has a decrease carbon footprint.

Also, to maintain cash on transportation, you may search for discounts and offers, inclusive of pupil or senior reductions for public transportation, or carpooling with coworkers to cut up the charge of gasoline.

Tips for keeping and repairing your automobile

Regularly take a look at and preserve your vehicle's fluids, which include oil, coolant, transmission fluid, and brake fluid.

Keep your tires well inflated and turned around, and take a look at the tread intensity regularly.

Regularly check and replace wiped out brake pads and rotors.

Have your automobile serviced regularly, following the manufacturer's encouraged time desk.

Keep an eye fixed constant for your automobile's warning lights, and address any troubles as fast as they seem.

Keep your automobile clean, every interior and out. This can assist extend the life of your vehicle's paint and upholstery.

Be aware about the not unusual issues which is probably associated with your automobile's make and version, and cope with them proactively.

Keep a report of all renovation and protection finished for your vehicle, together with the date, price, and mileage.

If you aren't comfortable appearing renovation yourself, it's miles exceptional to take your automobile to a professional mechanic to make certain that the protection are finished effectively.

Be aware about the guarantee in your vehicle and understand what it covers, in addition to the expiration date.

By following the ones recommendations, you can assist lengthen the life of your vehicle and keep it taking walks resultseasily.

How to shop coins on gasoline and public transportation

Plan your journeys: Combine errands and appointments to reduce the large form of trips you want to take.

Carpool: Consider carpooling with coworkers, pals or circle of relatives participants to cut up the value of fuel.

Use public transportation: Take gain of public transportation alternatives, inclusive of buses or trains, which may be cheaper than the use of.

Drive a gas-inexperienced car: Consider searching for a hybrid or electric powered automobile, which normally have better gas economic machine.

Maintain your car: Regularly take a look at and keep your automobile's fluids and tires, that may improve gas mileage.

Avoid rush hour: Try to keep away from riding at some stage in rush hour, at the same time as web site site visitors is heaviest and gas consumption is most.

Shop round for gas: Compare expenses of fuel station, to discover the most inexpensive one in your vicinity.

Use a loyalty card or cellular apps: Some gasoline stations offer loyalty applications or cellular apps that offer reductions on fuel.

Take benefit of reductions and offers: Look for reductions and offers, which includes pupil or senior discounts for public transportation, and stale-pinnacle fares.

Be aware of your driving conduct: Avoid aggressive using, like dashing, accelerating and braking , that may lower your gasoline mileage.

Public transportation and carpooling

Use public transportation: Take benefit of public transportation options, which includes buses, trains, and subways, which may be less high priced than riding, and additionally reduce web site traffic congestion and pollutants.

Look for discounts: Many cities provide reductions for university youngsters, seniors, and coffee-profits people.

Buy a month-to-month skip: If you operate public transportation frequently, it is able to be more rate-effective to shop for a monthly pass.

Use cell apps: Many towns have cellular apps that permit you to devise your adventure and buy tickets in advance.

Carpool: Consider carpooling with coworkers, buddies, or own family people to cut up the charge of gas and reduce the form of vehicles on the road.

Use a carpooling app: Use a carpooling app, like BlaBlaCar, to find human beings for your region who are using to the identical holiday spot.

Set up a carpool with coworkers: Coordinate with coworkers to set up a carpool schedule.

Take turns the use of: If you carpool frequently with the identical agency of people, take turns the use of to lessen the damage and tear and tear in your very personal automobile.

Planning a price range-fine excursion

Planning a fee variety-first-rate excursion may be hard, however it is virtually feasible. Here are some pointers that will help you plan a fee variety-quality excursion:

Set a budget: Determine how a bargain you may have sufficient cash to spend to your excursion and hold on with it.

Research places: Look for locations that provide right price to your cash.

Be flexible collectively together with your dates: Be bendy in conjunction with your tour dates, as airfare and resorts may be more high-priced at some point of peak adventure instances.

Look for offers: Keep a be careful for gives on airfare, lodges, and sports. Many airlines, hotels, and journey organizations offer discounts and specials at some stage in the one yr.

Book earlier: Book your flight and resort earlier to take advantage of early-fowl discounts.

Consider alternative hotels alternatives: Instead of staying in a lodge, do not forget unique hotels alternatives like vacation rentals, hostels, or tenting.

Eat like a close-by: Rather than eating at expensive consuming locations, try community avenue food, supermarkets and markets, it's far going to be cheaper and you may have the danger to flavor local meals.

Don't over plan: Avoid over-making plans your experience, so you have the power to take advantage of any closing-minute gives or reductions that you come across.

Avoid pinnacle season: If you may tour in the course of the off-season, you'll be capable of take advantage of lower prices.

Be aware about your spending: Be aware of your spending in the direction of your excursion, and attempt to persist with your charge variety as an entire lot as viable.

Chapter 4: Home And Utility Expenses

Energy-inexperienced living

Energy-inexperienced living entails making adjustments to the way you use energy in your private home as a way to reduce consumption and reduce your software bills.

One way to beautify electricity usual performance is through the use of power-green appliances.

These home equipment, which consist of fridges, washing machines, and air conditioners, are designed to apply much less electricity than trendy fashions.

Look for domestic system which may be licensed through way of the Energy Star software program, which suggests that they meet fantastic energy performance necessities set by way of the U.S. Environmental Protection Agency.

Another way to beautify energy standard performance is via implementing energy-saving behaviors. This can consist of factors like turning off lights and electronics even as they may be not in use, the use of herbal mild in preference to synthetic slight, and setting the thermostat to a decrease temperature inside the wintry climate and a higher temperature within the summer season.

There also are methods to apply renewable strength sources in your own home to lessen your strength consumption. This can include putting in sun panels or a small wind turbine to generate strength, the use of a geothermal warmth pump for heating and cooling, or installing a rainwater harvesting machine to reduce the quantity of water used for irrigation and exclusive family makes use of.

You also can decorate power efficiency through the use of making changes to the physical form of your private home. This can encompass things like sealing air leaks and collectively with insulation, planting wood or putting in shading devices to block the sun's rays inside the summer time, and putting in strength-efficient domestic home home windows and doors.

All these actions can help you to preserve giant amount of money on electricity costs, reduce your carbon footprint and make your own home more snug.

How to negotiate lease or mortgage payments

Negotiating hire or loan payments may be a complex device, but there are a few things you may do to boom your opportunities of achievement. Here are some guidelines to undergo in mind:

Do your research: Before you begin negotiating, accumulate information approximately the modern marketplace situations in your region. Look at similar rents or mortgage bills for comparable houses and use this information to help your case.

Be organized to provide an purpose to your economic situation: Landlords or mortgage creditors will need to recognize why you're asking for a reduction in lease or loan payments. Be organized to offer documentation that suggests your income and expenses, and offer an motive for any extenuating conditions which is probably affecting your capability to pay.

Be bendy: Consider supplying to make up the difference in lease or loan bills in certainly one of a kind procedures, which embody by means of agreeing to an extended hire or with the beneficial resource of creating additional maintenance to the property.

Be respectful and professional: Remember that you're soliciting for a choose, so it is important to be respectful and professional to your interactions with the landlord or mortgage lender. Be sincere and in advance about your scenario, and keep away from being confrontational or demanding.

Look for other options: If you are no longer capable of negotiate a reduction in rent or loan bills, undergo in thoughts searching out special housing alternatives, together with subletting or getting a roommate to percent expenses.

It's vital to be aware that the achievement of the negotiation will rely available available on the market situations, the financial state of affairs of the owner or loan lender, and the suitable instances of your scenario.

DIY domestic renovation

DIY home upkeep can be a wonderful manner to maintain money and enhance your dwelling area. However, it's miles critical to be sensible about your talents and boundaries, and to prioritize protection whilst venture any domestic protection. Here are some guidelines to endure in thoughts on the same time as planning DIY home maintenance:

Start small: If you are new to DIY domestic repairs, it's an excellent idea to start with easy obligations that allows you to assemble yourself notion and abilties. Examples encompass portray a room, changing a slight fixture, or fixing a leaky faucet.

Get informed: Before you start a DIY home restore task, make the effort to look at the tools and strategies you could need to finish the hobby. Watch online tutorials, take a look at books or articles, and trying to find recommendation from skilled DIYers.

Get the proper device: Having the right equipment for the task is important for any DIY domestic restore assignment. Make tremendous you have got all of the device you want before you begin, and spend money on correct great tools at the manner to closing.

Prioritize protection: Always placed on appropriate safety device, collectively with goggles and gloves, and take the important precautions to guard your self and others on the same time as working. Be privy to capacity risks, inclusive of electrical wiring, and in no manner take shortcuts in terms of protection.

Know your limits: While DIY domestic renovation may be a high-quality way to shop cash, it's miles crucial to realise your limits and to call in a professional while important. If you're uncertain approximately your capability to complete a restore very well or if the repair requires specialized competencies, it is first-rate to name in a professional.

By following the ones suggestions, you can nicely and efficiently adopt a huge form of DIY home protection, from smooth obligations to more complicated ones.

Chapter 5: Frugal Fashion And Personal Care

How to shop for garments on a price range

Look for income and clearance devices: Many shops regularly have earnings and clearance sections wherein you could discover gives on garments.

Shop at thrift and consignment stores: These stores regularly have a massive desire of lightly used clothes at a fragment of the charge of retail shops.

Buy fundamentals: Invest in essential, bendy portions that may be blended and coupled to create a number of garb.

Shop out of season: You can frequently discover brilliant offers on garments which might be out of season.

Use coupons and cut price codes: Many stores offer coupons and discount codes that may be done on your buy.

Be open to opportunity options: Consider purchasing for garments from opportunity assets alongside on-line marketplaces, 2nd-hand apps, or renting garments.

Check for terrific: Look for clothes which can be properly-made and function right tremendous fabric, with a purpose to last longer, saving you money ultimately.

Avoid rapid fashion: Try to avoid shopping for from fast-style manufacturers, which frequently produce clothes that crumble rapid and do now not keep as a notable deal as ordinary put on and tear.

Try DIY or upcycling: Get creative and try to repurpose or revamp clothes you already private, or buy garments which can be a bit too large or antique and turn them into some component new and fashionable.

Shop on-line: Online shopping can be a top notch way to discover offers and discounts, and there are numerous on-line stores focusing on finances-friendly garb.

Compare prices: Before growing a purchase, make the effort to examine charges across particular stores to ensure you are getting the tremendous deal.

Get innovative with layering: Invest in a few key portions, which encompass a flexible jacket or cardigan, that may be layered to create one-of-a-type seems.

Don't be afraid to buy secondhand: Buying secondhand clothes can be a terrific way to keep money and moreover lessen the environmental impact of rapid style.

Make use of apartment offerings: Renting garments can be a wonderful way to strive out new patterns or placed on style fashion designer clothing for unique activities at a fragment of the cost of buying them.

Be conscious of your non-public style: It's crucial to stick on your non-public style and now not definitely purchase clothes because of the reality they're on sale. You'll be lots less possibly to position on clothes you do no longer enjoy first rate in, regardless of how cheap they had been.

How to keep cash on hair and beauty products

Try preserve producers: Store-logo hair and splendor products can be truely as powerful as their more steeply-priced contrary numbers and might prevent cash.

Make your very own: Some hair and splendor merchandise can be made at domestic with additives located to your kitchen, like coconut oil, honey, and avocado.

Use multi-cause merchandise: Look for hair and splendor merchandise which have a couple of makes use of, which incorporates a shampoo that still doubles as a body wash, to preserve coins and reduce muddle.

Don't buy merchandise you do not want: Be aware about the products you are purchasing for and make sure you are not buying gadgets you don't really want.

Avoid impulse buys: Impulse buys can add up rapid, so attempt to face up to the temptation to buy products you do now not really want.

Take benefit of samples: Many splendor stores offer free samples of products. Ask the body of employees and they'll come up with samples of products you are inquisitive about in advance than purchasing for.

Use subscription services: Subscription services permit you to keep coins thru manner of delivering products to your door at normal intervals and frequently offer discounts for subscription individuals.

Look for gives and discounts (as explained formerly)

Shop on line (as defined formerly)

Compare prices (as described formerly)

Tips for retaining your cloth dresser

Organize your closet: Keep your garments prepared with the aid of shade, style, and occasion to make it smooth to locate what you need and keep song of what you've got were given had been given.

Keep a laundry time table: Laundry is a ordinary venture, so it's far vital to installation a agenda to preserve up with it, that manner you can not have a pile of dirty clothes and you will store coins on dry cleansing.

Repair and modify clothes: Instead of throwing away clothes that have a small tear or don't healthy pretty proper, consider getting them repaired or altered to increase their existence.

Store garments properly: Proper garage can help lengthen the lifestyles of your clothes, so ensure to shop them in a groovy, dry place, some distance from direct daylight and moisture.

Rotate your clothes: Instead of wearing the identical garments again and again, rotate them to give them a risk to relaxation and prevent located on and tear.

Clean and guard: Clean your garments frequently and use suitable care strategies collectively with dry cleaning or hand-washing, and use protectors for delicate fabric and shoes to keep them in proper situation.

Be conscious of care labels: Always examine the care labels for your clothes to ensure you are being involved for them well and not causing useless damage.

Invest in remarkable hangers: Good tremendous hangers can assist maintain your garments in shape and prevent stretching or misshaping of clothes.

Chapter 6: Entertainment On A Budget

How to discover unfastened or low-charge sports activities

Check out community network activities: Many cities and cities have loose events along with concert occasions, festivals, and farmer's markets which can be open to the general public.

Visit museums and libraries: Many museums and libraries offer unfastened or reduced-charge admission, and a few virtually have unfastened days or hours.

Take a hike: Going for a hike in a nearby park or nature reserve is a excellent way to revel in the outdoor freed from price.

Try DIY duties: You can try and make your non-public crafts, artwork, or DIY initiatives at domestic with materials you already have.

Have a picnic: Pack a lunch and experience a picnic in a close-by park or beach.

Utilize streaming services: You can discover an entire lot of unfastened or low-rate leisure on streaming offerings consisting of Netflix, Hulu, Amazon Prime Video and YouTube.

Volunteer: Many neighborhood corporations are constantly in need of volunteers, and you can have a look at new competencies on the equal time as giving decrease again in your network.

These are only some thoughts, but there are various extra techniques to discover loose or low-charge sports for entertainment on a charge range. Be present day and keep an open thoughts!

How to preserve coins on films, track, and books

Use streaming services: Streaming offerings like Netflix, Hulu, Amazon Prime Video, and Spotify provide a significant style of films, tune, and books at a month-to-month subscription fee this is generally a lot lots much less high-priced than shopping for or renting person titles.

Look for free of charge trials: Many streaming offerings provide loose trials, in order to assist you to get right of access to their content fabric fabric for a restricted time without paying.

Check out digital libraries: Many libraries now provide digital collections of e-books, audiobooks, and even films and track, which you can get proper of entry to for free of charge with a library card.

Buy used: You can frequently find extremely good deals on used films, music, and books, each in physical shops and on-line.

Listen to track without charge: Online structures like Spotify and YouTube have quite a few unfastened tune to take note of.

Rent as an alternative of purchasing: You can lease films and books from community libraries or online rental offerings like Redbox or Kindle Unlimited.

Look for reductions and deals: Keep a be careful for income, discounts, and other gives on movies, tune, and books, each online and in bodily stores.

Use coupons: You also can look for coupons and promo codes to get reductions to your purchase.

Keep in thoughts that these are only some methods to save coins on films, tune, and books. Be high-quality to check prices and options to find the first-class offers for you.

How to revel in a night day out without breaking the financial institution

Have a potluck night meal: Invite friends over and ask every body to supply a dish to percent. This way, you'll all get to revel in a fun night time day out collectively without spending plenty of cash on meals.

Host a game night time time: Gather your friends and characteristic a exercise night time at domestic, wherein you can all play video games and enjoy each other's organization without cost.

Go for a stroll: A terrific stroll with friends in a park or seaside is a top notch manner to enjoy the out of doors and spend time together without spending cash.

Have a movie night time: Invite buddies over and pick out a film to have a look at collectively. This is a extraordinary way to revel in a night day trip with out spending a variety of cash on tickets or concessions.

Try a BYOB (Bring Your Own Bottle) eating place: Many restaurants let you supply your non-public bottle of wine or beer, that could save you coins on beverages.

Take gain of unfastened occasions in your place: take a look at the calendar of activities in your city, lots of them offer loose or low-fee sports activities which incorporates outside stay shows, gala's, and theater performances.

Look for gives: Many consuming locations, bars, and exclusive agencies provide specials and reductions on wonderful nights of the week, so make certain to test for offers earlier than you head out.

Be innovative: Be progressive and think out of the field, you could plan a a laugh night day experience via manner of performing some trouble you have in no way accomplished in advance than, whether or no longer it is a cooking elegance, a minutiae night time time or a karaoke night time.

Remember, a night out couldn't should be highly-priced to be exciting. With touch creativity and planning, you could have a laugh with buddies without breaking the monetary institution.

Chapter 7: Traveling Frugally

How to devise a budget-incredible vacation

Set a price range: Determine how masses coins you may provide you with the money for to spend in your excursion and keep on with it.

Research locations: Look for destinations that offer a first rate stability of affordability and activities.

Look for gives: Keep a be careful for offers on flights, accommodations, and sports. Sign up for e-mail newsletters from airlines and excursion web sites to stay informed about sales and reductions.

Consider opportunity lodges: Instead of reserving a hotel, recall staying in a vacation condominium or camping.

Plan in advance: Book flights and lodges properly earlier to take benefit of early chicken discounts.

Pack well: Avoid overpacking and convey satisfactory the requirements to hold on baggage fees.

Be aware of meals expenses: Plan to cook dinner dinner your very very own meals or devour at neighborhood street agencies to keep coins on meals.

Take advantage of public transportation: Walking and public transportation can be a amazing way to shop cash even as also experiencing the community lifestyle.

Be open to new evaluations: Don't get too stuck up in sticking to a strict itinerary. Be open to new testimonies and take advantage of free or less expensive sports.

How to shop cash on airfare and lodging

Book in advance: Book your flights and accommodations well earlier to take gain of early chicken discounts.

Be flexible together with your tour dates: Consider travelling within the path of the low season or midweek to hold money.

Use flight evaluation net websites: Use flight evaluation internet web websites inclusive of Kayak, Expedia, or Google Flights to assess prices across multiple airlines.

Consider change airports: Look into flying into opportunity airports that may be close by your vacation spot.

Sign up for electronic mail symptoms: Sign up for electronic mail indicators from airways and journey web web sites to stay knowledgeable approximately income and reductions.

Look for package gives: Consider reserving a package deal deal that includes flights and motels.

Use a excursion rewards credit score rating score card: Use a excursion rewards credit score rating rating card to earn elements or miles that can be redeemed for flights or hotel stays.

How to make the maximum of your journey price range

Prioritize your fees: Decide which sports activities sports and reviews are most critical to you and allocate your rate variety because of this.

Research and plan in advance: Research your excursion spot to find out free or low-fee sports activities, and plan earlier to take benefit of discounts and gives.

Use public transportation: Use public transportation to store on transportation expenses and moreover enjoy the close by manner of existence.

Eat like a nearby: Look for close by avenue vendors or markets to strive real and occasional-fee food.

Shop as it need to be: Take advantage of network markets and souvenir shops to find out offers and specific, regionally-made products.

Avoid height seasons: Avoid touring during top seasons while costs will be predisposed to be higher.

Use generation for your advantage: Use apps or internet web sites to discover deals on sports, transportation, and inns.

Avoid foreign coins conversion prices: Use credit rating or debit cards that do not charge forex conversion expenses and moreover withdraw cash from ATMs that do not charge prices.

Be privy to your spending: Keep music of your spending within the path of your adventure and make adjustments as vital to stay inner your price range.

Chapter 8: Saving For The Future

To create an economic financial financial savings plan, hold in thoughts the subsequent steps:

Determine your economic savings goals - what do you want to buy and thru even as?

Assess your contemporary economic situation - how a lot coins do you presently have and what are your costs?

Create a price range - pick out out regions wherein you could cut again on costs to free up coins for financial financial savings.

Set up automated transfers - installation for a part of your income to be robotically transferred right into a savings account.

Review and modify your plan as wished - as your economic state of affairs adjustments, evaluation your plan and adjust it because of this.

Consider a economic savings account or investment account to develop your cash.

It's critical to keep in mind that economic financial savings plans require discipline and consistency. Stick for your plan and make modifications as important to ensure you gain your dreams.

How to set financial dreams

Setting monetary goals will allow you to interest your efforts and make development within the direction of attaining your monetary aspirations. Here are some steps that will help you set monetary goals:

Identify what you need to accumulate: This might be a specific buy, which encompass a residence or vehicle, or a extra massive purpose, which include saving for retirement or paying off debt.

Make your goals particular and measurable: For instance, in place of announcing "I need to shop coins," say "I want to keep $20,000 for a down fee on a residence within the subsequent 2 years."

Set a practical time frame: Be sensible approximately how lengthy it'll take to achieve your goal and set a cut-off date for yourself.

Prioritize your desires: Decide which dreams are maximum critical to you and popularity on them first.

Create a route of action: Break down your intention into smaller steps and create a plan to benefit every step.

Track your improvement: Keep music of your development and make changes as wanted.

Review and regulate your dreams: As your times trade, evaluate and alter your wants to make certain they're nonetheless applicable and feasible.

Setting monetary goals is an ongoing manner, and also you need to frequently compare and modify your desires to make sure they live relevant and feasible. And additionally, preserve in thoughts that it is proper to have short term and long time goals.

How to create an emergency fund

An emergency fund is a monetary financial savings account set aside for sudden fees, which include interest loss, clinical bills, or home upkeep. Here are a few steps that will help you create an emergency fund:

Determine how a good deal you want: A sizeable rule of thumb is to have three to 6 months' really certainly really worth of living costs saved in an emergency fund.

Calculate your costs for an normal month, along aspect rent/loan, utilities, transportation, food, and one of a kind necessities, and multiply that quantity by means of using the huge form of months you need to have saved.

Set up a dedicated account: Open a savings account specifically on your emergency fund and installation automatic transfers from your financial institution account to this account.

Make ordinary contributions: Consistency is essential whilst building an emergency fund. Decide on an quantity you may correctly maintain each month and installation automatic transfers or make everyday contributions for your emergency fund account.

Keep it liquid: An emergency fund ought to be handy on the same time as you want it, so pick out a financial economic financial savings account or cash market fund this is resultseasily available and has little to no effects for withdrawing rate variety.

Review and modify: Review your emergency fund frequently and alter your economic financial savings plan as wished.

Avoid the usage of it for non-emergency costs: Only use your emergency fund for surprising charges, and strive now not to dip into it for non-emergency expenses.

Building an emergency fund takes time and consistency, but it's miles actually really worth it ultimately to have a safety internet for unexpected expenses.

How to invest cash on a first rate fee range

Start small: Even small quantities of cash can be invested over time and grow to be massive quantities. Consider starting with a small sum of money every month, which include $25 or $50.

Take advantage of dollar-fee averaging: By making an investment a hard and fast amount of money on a everyday time table, regardless of the inventory fee, you may take advantage of greenback-charge averaging. This will will will let you avoid searching for at the pinnacle of the market and as an possibility buy at a lower rate over time.

Invest in low-fee index fee range: Index funds are a type of mutual fund that pastimes to in shape the overall performance of a specific stock market index. These finances are typically low-fee and may be a top notch alternative for buyers on a respectable fee range.

Consider robo-advisors: Robo-advisors are online investment systems that use algorithms to govern your investments. They regularly have low minimal funding requirements and occasional expenses, that can purpose them to a remarkable alternative for price range-conscious customers.

Look without cost investment alternatives: Some groups provide unfastened funding alternatives, which includes free inventory searching for and selling systems or free inventory giveaways for signing up. These unfastened alternatives can be a exquisite manner to make investments small portions of cash with out incurring considerable charges.

Educate yourself: Investing can appear daunting, but with the beneficial aid of educating yourself, you can make extra knowledgeable funding selections. Look for free of charge assets such as on line articles, podcasts, or webinars to analyze more approximately making an funding.

Remember, making an investment is an prolonged-term technique, or maybe small investments can increase through the years with normal contributions and compounding impact. It's additionally critical to diversify your investments, and preserve in thoughts the hazard-reward ratio as properly.

Chapter 9: Staying Induced

Finding stability

Staying prompted whilst dwelling a frugal way of life may be tough, as it can require making sacrifices and avoiding impulse purchases. However, it is crucial to endure in thoughts the reasons why you have decided on to live frugally, which incorporates saving for a specific intention or decreasing debt.

One way to live stimulated is to set specific dreams for you. Whether it's far saving for a vacation, a down price on a residence or paying off credit score rating rating card debt, having a smooth and precise intention in mind can assist hold you impacted.

Another way to stay endorsed is to locate balance. It is vital to now not absolutely deprive yourself of the property you revel in, along with eating out or searching for. Instead, find out stability amongst indulging in small luxuries and sticking on your fee variety.

It additionally may be beneficial to discover a community of like-minded folks who percentage the same values and may help and inspire every other in living frugally. Joining a frugal residing organization or dialogue board can offer duty and motivation to stick to your dreams.

In all staying stimulated in a frugal way of life calls for locating stability, putting particular desires, and surrounding yourself with a supportive network.

Making frugal residing a way of existence

Making frugal residing a manner of lifestyles calls for a shift in mind-set and conduct Here are some pointers to help make frugal living a sustainable manner of existence:

Prioritize your spending: Before making any purchase, ask yourself if it is a need or a want. Prioritize your spending on crucial gadgets, consisting of meals and housing, and decrease or dispose of spending on non-vital objects.

Create a finances: Having a rate range in place allows you to music your spending and find out regions in which you could cut again.

Shop clever: Compare fees and search for earnings and discounts while seeking out groceries and excellent objects. Consider shopping for used devices or choosing general manufacturers to keep cash.

Live interior your technique: Avoid overspending and dwelling beyond your technique Instead, attention on dwelling internal your way and saving on your future.

Be privy to your electricity utilization: Reduce your power consumption with the useful resource of turning off lighting fixtures and domestic device even as not in use, using strength-inexperienced home equipment, and being privy to your water usage.

Find opportunity varieties of leisure: Instead of going out to steeply-priced consuming locations or movies, find alternative varieties of entertainment, together with trekking, picnicking, or trying out new recipes at domestic.

Be aware of your waste: Reducing waste not exceptional saves coins however also allows the environment. Consider recycling, composting, and reusing gadgets rather of buying new ones.

Making frugal living a way of existence requires a willpower to being privy to your spending and making conscious alternatives that align at the side of your values. With time and effort, it turns into a herbal and sustainable manner of existence.

Next steps for persevered savings

Once you've got were given installed a frugal life-style and feature seen some financial financial savings, it's miles important to preserve finding techniques to preserve cash. Here are a few next steps for endured financial savings:

Automate financial economic financial savings: Set up automated monetary financial savings transfers from your bank account in your monetary economic savings account every month. This will assist you keep without even thinking about it.

Revisit your charge range: Review your fee range frequently and make modifications as needed. Identify regions in which you could reduce again further and don't forget increasing your financial financial savings dreams.

Shop smarter: Look for techniques to hold cash on ordinary fees along facet groceries, bills and utilities by way of manner of seeking out reductions, coupons, and offers.

Invest in your destiny: Consider investing in a retirement plan or one-of-a-type lengthy-term economic savings account to ensure a solid monetary destiny.

Prioritize debt repayment: If you've got superb debt, prioritize paying it off as fast as possible. The an awful lot tons less debt you have got, the extra cash you may ought to store.

Shop for a better deal: examine expenses and charges for offerings together with vehicle insurance, cellular cellphone plans, and internet provider agencies.

Avoid impulse looking for: Take time to count on earlier than creating a purchase, and avoid impulse looking for via growing a listing of things you need and sticking to it.

Be revolutionary: search for present day techniques to keep which incorporates bartering, swapping, or freelancing to earn more money.

Continuing to shop coins requires determination and attempt, but with the proper mind-set and techniques, it is able to be a sustainable and profitable part of your lifestyle.

How to keep a frugal way of life inside the long term

Maintaining a frugal way of life in the long time requires consistency and backbone. Here are a few suggestions that will help you preserve a frugal lifestyle in the prolonged-term:

Make frugality a addiction: Incorporate frugal behavior into your every day everyday, which include meal planning, budgeting, and shopping for gives.

Stay stimulated: Remind yourself of the reasons why you selected a frugal life-style, which incorporates saving for a particular cause or reducing debt.

Be adaptable: Be willing to make modifications and adapt to new conditions. For instance, if your earnings adjustments, modify your price range therefore.

Keep studying: Stay knowledgeable approximately new techniques to maintain coins and be open to gaining know-how of new competencies, consisting of a way to prepare dinner or a way to keep your very personal vehicle.

Track your improvement: Keep music of your spending and financial savings to appearance how a ways you've got come and to live advocated.

Avoid temptations : Surround yourself with individuals who manual your way of life and keep away from situations which can tempt you to overspend.

Prioritize your values: Stay actual for your values and make certain your spending aligns with what is maximum critical to you.

Be affected character: Remember that a frugal lifestyle is a marathon, no longer a dash, and that it takes time to see the benefits.

Maintaining a frugal manner of existence within the lengthy-time period requires consistency, adaptability, and staying power, but with the right thoughts-set and techniques, it can be a sustainable and worthwhile manner of lifestyles.

Additional sources for saving cash

Budgeting apps: There are many budgeting apps to be had that allow you to track your spending, create a price variety, and preserve cash. Some popular apps encompass Mint, PocketGuard, and Wally.

Coupon websites: Websites which encompass RetailMeNot, Coupons.Com, and Groupon offer discounts and coupons for a massive form of products and services.

Price assessment web sites: Websites along facet PriceGrabber, Kayak, and Shopzilla can help you examine fees on a whole lot of services and products.

Personal finance blogs: Personal finance blogs together with Get Rich Slowly, Frugal Rules, and Wise Bread provide recommendations and advice on the manner to shop cash and manage your rate variety.

Public libraries: Public libraries provide a huge sort of assets, consisting of books on private finance, budgeting, and frugal dwelling.

Online groups: Join on line companies along side Reddit's Frugal subreddit or Facebook companies devoted to frugal dwelling to proportion pointers and get recommendation from others.

Government resources: Government net web websites along side Benefits.Gov and Consumer.Gov offer facts on economic help applications and customer protection prison guidelines.

Professional recommendation: Consult with a monetary representative or accountant to get expert recommendation at the manner to save cash and manage your fee variety.

Bargain looking: search for garage income, thrift shops, and advertisements for remarkable gives.

DIY competencies: Learn a way to repair, keep, and improve matters on your personal, this can save you from having to shop for new items or pay for steeply-priced services.

These assets can be very useful in supporting you analyze new approaches to maintain cash and make clever economic selections.

Chapter 10: The Financial Minimalist Mindset

Changing Perceptions of Wealth

When it entails coins, we frequently examine ourselves to extraordinary people. As you scroll thru social media, you be conscious humans located up subject approximately their travels, satisfied existence, and pleasure in having the capability to shop for this and that. However, what you don't see is the behind-the-scenes of ways they received those matters. It could be brilliant to take into account that what you fee differs from others. I realize someone who owns many Hermes Birkin luggage however has no coins to hire a attorney at the same time as she gets a DUI. I additionally recognize someone on the polar contrary of this shape of man or woman who cuts up his toothpaste tube to scrape off the final paste while he can't squeeze a few thing out of it. Thankfully, I don't have severa polar contrary human beings in my lifestyles. I live via the terms of motivational speaker Jim Rohn, "You are the not unusual of the five people you spend the maximum time with." I surround myself with the people I take delivery of as actual with percentage the identical dreams and values as me and those who place their importance on friendship and time spent together to cultivate studies. They all have considered one of type income stages, however even as selecting what to spend money on, they do not need to waste their cash on luxury manufacturers. If they do purchase a high-priced item, it's miles a praise for his or her tough paintings and a few component they'll manage to pay for on pinnacle of their requirements. We'll dive extra into this detail while we get to Chapter 2.

There will normally be people with extra cash than you. If you hold comparing yourself to what special humans have, you'll in no way be satisfied with what you have.

The quickest way to be broke is in case you keep spending coins to show different humans how a great deal you have got. I hate to break it to you, however at the cease of the day, no individual cares approximately you greater than your self.

You ought to determine out what is sufficient for you. I moreover use a trick to check the alternative give up of the spectrum. Instead of searching at the people with some of cash, I do not forget people with little to no cash. I understand I stated now not to study, but I need to recognize each ends of the spectrum to determine what I anticipate is enough for my circle of relatives and me to thrive.

Ask your self the following questions:

1.   What are my payments each month?

2.   What is my cutting-edge lifestyle?

3.   What might my life-style appear like in 1, five, 10 years? Do I want a

smaller/larger house? Do I need children? Should I shop up so I certainly have sufficient to deliver my kids to the university of their choice?

four. What desires to exchange to advantage my future way of lifestyles?

5.   What do I want in existence? What do I need in lifestyles?

By answering the ones questions, you can alternate your belief of wealth and decide out your plan with the cash you currently have. Chapter 2 will cowl budgeting strategies to reap your 1, 5, and 10-one year goals.

Embracing Simplicity: How Simplifying Finances Lead to Contentment.

If there's something I certainly have found from my journey to being debt-free, keeping subjects easy is probably on the pinnacle of the listing. Simplicity is vital to attaining massive desires. If you harm complicated troubles into small portions, you could accomplish them quicker with small wins. Even if you fail on the ones small components of your approach, you simply will fail speedy and recognise what to "not" do more fast than those looking for to recuperation the problem multi feature chunk. Consequently, you'll adapt and provide you with new strategies earlier than they do. If topics are too complex, you maximum possibly will procrastinate and no longer do them. Well, the same idea applies on your charge variety. It might be awesome to start through doing small, smooth every day subjects to look modifications to your fee variety. Starting small and preserving it easy is the essential factor to long-time period success.

Chapter 11: Building A Minimalist Budget

Financial Goals: Reflect on Your Financial Goals

Directing time and power to the topics I price brings pleasure to my family and me. In choosing to have a look at this e-book, you are already one step earlier of the crowd because of the truth you recognize a trouble exists. Still, you need assist seeing what can also need to limit your circulate closer to your financial goals. If you do, you can need validation that your way is the right/incorrect manner to head about it. Setting monetary goals may be clean. There should be quick-term, mid-term, and prolonged-time period desires in area. If you aren't running within the direction of setting your monetary dreams, you may be spending extra money than you have to. You will then be stuck in the debt cycle and feel you in no manner have sufficient. It will maximum likely depart you greater prone and insecure.

I grew up in a own family enthusiastic about "making" cash. All we concept about become to make more, and additional became higher. My dad and mom in no way taken into consideration "financial savings," so my brother and I had been by no means savers. You bet we're fantastic spenders. Our own family spent plenty that we had no cash to pay our energy and water payments. We may want to sleep within the darkish, bloodless room to get with the aid of using the usage of in the course of these times. On days on the equal time because the water modified into approximately to get reduce off, we might have buckets of water set aside to get with the resource of. Eviction notices are absolutely every other piece of paper on our door. Forget about credit score rating gambling playing playing cards; we didn't have any. We did not healing the trouble from the middle. We were getting ready to having no roof over our heads and no vehicle to get us to our jobs.

Then I began out to count on, what the heck is inaccurate with how we do things? I then scoured the internet and severa books to educate myself on cash. A few years later, I am glad to mention that I am sooner or later out of that cycle, and my ardour is to help others get out of that cycle as properly. I have been given out of it through installing my short-term, mid-time period, and prolonged-time period plans.

To set your expectancies right away, changing your coins behavior will not show up in a single day. Most of this e-book will cognizance on building brief-term desires and practices as a manner to in the end assemble appropriate behavior that allows you to translate right right into a high-quality mid to prolonged-term plan.

As an exercising, consider the lowest monetary day of your existence. Do you want to be in that characteristic day after today? If you've got got kids, do you want your children to experience that? Do you need to live paycheck-to-paycheck for the rest of your lifestyles?

Your lowest financial day can also/might not be as extreme as mine, but we need to begin somewhere. Our short-time period purpose placing will assist us similarly mirror on our coins scenario. We have to set a charge variety, reduce our debt, and create an emergency fund.

Understanding Needs vs. Wants: Highlighting the Basics of Spending.

Determining Needs

Financial necessities are prices which might be required in an effort to stay and art work. They are the recurrent expenses in all likelihood to eat a massive part of your profits – mortgage, lease, and automobile coverage.

Sample List of Needs: Housing, Utility (e.G., power, water, fuel), Transportation (e.G., vehicle, bus, metro, and so forth.), Insurance, Food

Determining Wants

Wants are charges that make your lifestyles a great deal much less complex. They are gadgets offered for enjoyment or interest. You may additionally need to stay without them, but they make your existence greater thrilling. For instance, eating is a want, but every day lunches out are much more likely a want.

Sample List of Wants: Travel, Entertainment (e.G., Netflix, Hulu, Disney+, and so forth.), Designer garb or greater apparel in enormous, Gym memberships, Specialty Coffee (e.G., Starbucks)

Everyone's want and desires might be extraordinary. You also can furthermore need a car to tour to and from paintings every day, however the sort of vehicle you require may additionally change. A top magnificence automobile can be important in case your hobby wishes you to strength spherical immoderate-powered customers. If you use the auto to in reality tour to and from paintings, a far plenty less high priced automobile will suffice.

The identical is authentic for smaller-rate fee tag purchases, which embody that new jacket you've had your eye on. Outerwear is critical to guard you from the factors. Still, if you have already got three jackets, that jacket is certainly a need.

Setting Aside Money for Both Needs and Wants

My non-public enjoy helped me understand that I need to attention on my desires first and, therefore, that turned into what I prioritized.

Let's start thru inclusive of need and desires to your budget.

Step 1: List

To start, make a listing of the entirety you buy. That covers the whole lot, even lifestyles coverage and relaxation room paper. After that, classify your purchases into huge training like coverage, cable, and the cellphone. If you may't endure in mind, have a take a look at your financial organization and credit rating card statements for the beyond three months. Online banking gadget are really higher than earlier than at maintaining apart spending classes. Even if the algorithm is wrong, you could continually recategorize it manually.

Step 2: Categorize

Separate the types into two organizations: want and desires. Insurance and a critical mobile phone plan are requirements, regardless of the fact that a Netflix subscription and a pinnacle charge television package deal deal are probably desires.

Step 3: Prioritize

Add up the totals, then set your priorities.

Step four: Needs and Wants

Lay it all out and function an honest verbal exchange with yourself approximately what you want and need.

I am a huge fan of paper and pencil. By physically writing it down, the whole lot will become more concrete.

Here is an instance of in reality the prices that I prioritize. They are the subjects I need to pay to stay my modern-day-day way of lifestyles. My list may be high-quality from yours as we've were given terrific spending needs.

Mortgage or Rent

Mortgage or Renter Insurance

Utilities (fuel, electric powered powered, and water)

Car (price, insurance, gas, oil modifications, preservation)

Health Insurance & Medical Expenses

Food

Savings

Cellphone

Internet

Credit card #1

Credit card #2 (pay the very excellent hobby one first; once completed, CUT UP THE CARD and pass immediately to credit score score card #3 and so on) Now, allow's have a study the charges that I removed.

Chapter 12: Frugal Living Practices

Living Cheaply Without Being Cheap – Frugal Living Practices, My Favorite Topic to Talk About

Minimalist Home and Lifestyle: Tips on Reducing Clutter

Beyond your bank account, minimalist living profoundly influences all aspects of our lives, which includes our homes. Adopting a minimalist life-style and residence includes more than without a doubt clearing litter; it is also designing a setting that exudes intentionality, simplicity, and freedom from extraneous expenses and subjects. At first, it could sound overwhelming, but the extra you declutter, the more it becomes a addiction.

I slowly started out my minimalist journey as soon as I met my husband eleven years inside the past. It is one of the many motives I married him. His circle of relatives labeled him a cheapskate and continuously joked that his cash may quick have mould growing on it if he didn't use it. But then, as I seemed closer, he modified into now not as stingy as each person idea. He spent coins on the topics he pretty valued, like setting out with buddies and consuming real meals. He modified into the other of me, no matter the truth that, regarding cash. His family became all approximately "financial monetary financial savings" and no longer "spending." They could expect long and hard about every dollar they had been about to spend. In cross returned, they usually had cash in their account, a roof over their head, food at the table, and plenty of others. In our circle of relatives, we might purchase furniture as soon as for domestic decorations, and that's it. The rest have been donations from people who preferred beautifying their homes and favored to remove their antique subjects. We normally concept about "reasonably-priced and unfastened" and repurposed gadgets to use throughout the residence earlier than looking for. Our philosophy became (and although is), if it doesn't harm, then why change?

Now this isn't to mention that you need to now not beautify your own home. You want to pick the right subjects to buy that would enhance the appearance of your space with out taking on too much of the real assets. Recently, I in reality have moreover picked up a DIY home renovation hobby. I grew uninterested in our blue and crimson flowered wallpaper, so I peeled it all off myself and repainted the walls with a lighter tone. Having worked on patching the wall after the wallpaper became taken off have grow to be this shape of ache inside the butt, so I developed a addiction of not placing a few issue at the partitions when you do not forget that then because of the reality I didn't need to interrupt all my tough paintings. When someone comes into our home, they continually suppose that my husband and I truly moved in due to the truth we've got many empty walls and living regions. We snort out loud and inform our site visitors that it is straightforward to smooth the house this manner. We discover it impossible to resist.

Why have to you want to lessen muddle?

There are many reasons to reduce litter. Three important motives are to attention better, reduce strain so there's much less to easy, and visually increase the size of your living.

How to do it?

1.   Remove belongings you don't use each day from the kitchen counter and dwelling area.

2.   Move food to the pantry or shelves.

3.   Remove vain decor, kids' stuff, cookbooks, souvenirs, and magnets/pix from your fridge. Have a very precise vicinity for these items in your home.

four. Simplify wall decor. A top-best picture is ok however keep away from too colourful of history landscapes and art work. Instead, use impartial shades. Stick to white and impartial-colored walls, curtains, and so forth. These colors are timeless.

5.	Establish regulations for toys in the house, like no toys inside the dwelling room, or designate a play place. Limit the amount of toys your kids have. Seriously, it doesn't take masses to entertain them.

If You Don't Use It, Monetize It.

Often, I would monetize the donated devices received from friends. I did the identical problem with gadgets I offered as part of my impulse buy. I am human, anyhow. Poshmark is my drift-to for promoting apparel and footwear, and I use Facebook Marketplace for promoting extraordinary junk. I am easy, so I stick with web websites. Most regularly, someone will in the long run buy the gadgets if the submit exists prolonged enough. You can do the same issue with the gadgets across the residence. Look for devices you have not touched in years. This is a sign that they want to move.

Personal Attachments to Stuff

My father is this sort of hoarder. He loves looking for and hoarding. We have a 34-one year-old Electone keyboard that he despite the fact that refuses to allow cross. It's virtually sitting and gathering dust. I realise I cannot get him out of the purchasing for and hoarding cycle until I change myself and show him how I do it. I use him as an instance for me to do the opportunity. I recognize I do not need to be like him when I grow to be antique, so I want to do some factor he didn't do whilst he became greater more youthful. I love him dearly; there can be a bond I keep dear among my dad and mom and me. I dare say that the whole thing I am building nowadays is for them.

Regardless, some conduct are simply tough to break.

You possibly have similar examples in life, too, one way or each different. It doesn't need to be your parents. It can be each person you understand who you don't want to grow to be like. See how they live their lives and do the opportunity.

Smart Consumer Choices: How to Shop and Live Frugally Without Sacrificing Quality

I commenced to stay with the principle of wondering myself before shopping for. I supplied myself a $1,three hundred Gucci handbag five years inside the past, and little did I apprehend, I without a doubt have used it tons much less than ten times. My silly beyond has led me to grow to be a more frugal man or woman these days. It takes time to earn cash, and my time is freedom. Using this coins now approach I am chipping away at my freedom in the destiny. For example, earlier than I purchase a donut, I query, "Is this one donut really worth $1.29 of my freedom?" The equal software program applies to a bigger buy like a brand new automobile. I ask myself, "Is this Lexus properly truly worth $50,000 of my freedom once I can get a Toyota Corolla for $23,000? What's my quit purpose with this purchase? Is it to stress from aspect A to issue B? Then, need to I get a modern-day car? Why now not a secondhand car?" Thoughts can skip on and on. Thinking like this has substantially changed how I experience about buying.

I am conscious that not the entirety cheap is good and no longer everything expensive is lousy. If you interest on searching out reasonably-priced however no longer pleasant, you will maintain shopping for reasonably-priced each month considering that some factor you buy will go to waste. Subsequently, a reasonably-priced purchase should price you greater over the long time, and you don't need that. Buying an lousy lot much less but higher is how we are capable of make a frugal, sustainable, and genuinely satisfied life-style. You don't want to begin seeking out jeans beneath $20 or keep away from eating out the least bit fees. Those topics are not sustainable and could flip you proper right into a grumpy person.

The factors that pass into smart spending are price and rate. If you want to save extra cash in recent times, you need to begin thinking about the rate of the acquisition and not clearly the price tag. Warren Buffett as soon as said, "Price is what you pay. Value is what you get." Furthermore, values are subjective and variety from individual to man or woman.

Let's have a take a look at an example.

Imagine you want to shop for a settee for masses plenty less coins. There are alternatives: one for $500 and the other for $2,000. Simply accepting the less costly offer will result in a $1,500 monetary financial savings.

But what takes vicinity whilst we add fee to the equation?

What if the $500 sofa is from a reasonably-priced business enterprise and the couch will fast start to disintegrate, whilst a enterprise that makes the $2,000 sofa, might be comfortable and ultimate for at the least 10+ years? Did you get the higher deal if you purchased the "a good deal much less highly-priced" sofa however didn't revel in the use of it as lots and had to update it extra often? Imagine that!

Does that imply we must generally strive for costly, excessive-charge items and services if low-charge, low-charge gadgets are a lousy use of coins?

No, now not constantly. The sofa example demonstrates why it is important to disentangle the concepts of price and rate. When you don't forget each requirements, sticking on your financial targets is less difficult. It does now not mean that reasonably-priced purchases are commonly an issue, each. The preference to keep cash in advance can also make you revel in frugal. Still, this may regularly encourage you to complete later purchases to complement or update inferior items.

Social Media

Be honest with yourself, how an entire lot time do you spend on Twitter, Facebook, Instagram, TikTok, and YouTube each day? Social media as a advertising and marketing, earnings, and consumer dating control tool has shifted from vital manufacturers to mom-and-pop stores on Main Street over the last ten years. It taps into our overly robust or poorly confined dreams, preoccupations, or moves related to shopping and spending, negatively affecting our wallets.

I absolutely have these kind of social media debts, too. I observe inclinations and posts which might be applicable to me. However, I try and distance myself from posting some thing. My Instagram account has an lousy lot less than ten images/testimonies approximately me. The relaxation got here from friends tagging me. I in no way publish on TikTok however great have it to appearance posts that pals ship to signify specific meals. I use Facebook to be part of groups that percent comparable pursuits as I do. I sincerely have money owed like absolutely everyone else, but I am consciously selective approximately what I put up and study thru the various structures.

For starters, preventing posting matters about your self on social media can help you avoid taking place social media web sites inside the first vicinity. When you save you posting things about your self, you will not want to test on others. Do you care about specific posts, or do you need them to look what you do to show them which you are doing some factor comparable, too? I take a look at on my buddy's nicely-being once in a while however don't spend hours scrolling endlessly. My actual buddies are folks that textual content or name me for my part on my mobile cellphone.

Once you've got were given shaved off a few hours of social media from your life, you may observe that you can not be a victim of commercials explicitly tailor-made for your age organization, earnings level, and geographic area.

Here is my caveat. Not all advertisements are awful. Some commercials on my feed are useful educational-smart for me. Hence, I float there each sometimes for my edification. I assume this is wherein your judgment will come into play.

Cost Effective Travel

Some of us have tour aspirations and love experiencing particular locations. I am one in every of them. It might be a mistake to count on that minimalists are homebodies, cloistered in their humble abodes for worry that inside the occasion that they assignment out into the area, it's going to cause spending tension to get up. Some humans like to spend their amusement and vacation time spherical domestic, at the identical time as others need to peer the arena. Regarding tour, minimalism focuses more at the planning problem of factors. The quicker you plan and feature a hard and fast itinerary, the better you may estimate and manipulate your excursion prices.

I keep away from getting excursion programs just like the plague. I make it a assignment to find the great gives and plan to get my itinerary much less pricey than the excursion packages.

Planning My Itinerary Ahead of Time

I normally start my are seeking out thru looking on the itinerary of the specific excursions for the holiday spot. Because I am planning, I without a doubt have a desire to choose and pick out out the sports. I may need to use the ones pre-made itineraries as a starter and make adjustments from there. For motels, I may additionally want to have a look at my itinerary and ebook low-priced places close to the web sites I'm touring. It doesn't must be five stars, but it should be clean. I would pay greater to live in the direction of the web sites than further away as I am additionally factoring within the rate of transportation. I go together with a few aspect makes experience for car rentals and discover the best gives on line. Some agency jobs offer tour reductions for bookings. The timing of even as to go on excursion additionally performs a sizeable element in my making plans. Off-season tour is once I locate the great good deal and plenty less crowds. But in case you can't journey low season, even an afternoon or distinction out of your meant instances can prevent cash on airfares, motels, and rental automobiles.

Packing

As a person who practices minimalist dwelling, I generally journey with only a deliver-on. I am no longer an influencer, so I don't need to appear to be the ones Insta-pix with beautiful flowing apparel, hats, and makeup. I'm positive spenders love searching for new garments for their journey. I tried not to fall into that vicious spending dependancy cycle once more. I % whatever I already have, plus a small bottle of detergent to smooth my clothes in the inn room. For a virtual virtual digital camera, I use my smartphone. For toiletries, I % subjects in small bottles to get thru TSA. I do have one excessive-upkeep request at some point of packing: to ensure I in reality have the shampoo, conditioner, and pores and skin care of my choice. Please don't decide; all of us have our doggy peeves.

Food

For food, I generally pass wherein the locals bypass, actually so permits with my meals price range extraordinarily. I'm not so obsessed with Michelin-big call or 5-celebrity eating places every. I typically consider the fee and rate spending elements as my precedence. I attempt to ebook motels that embody complimentary breakfast. It doesn't ought to be whatever grand, just sufficient to stay complete until lunch. The heavy meals are generally at lunch and no longer dinner. The fees for dinner are commonly better than lunch expenses. For dinner, I may additionally carry out a little component moderate and smooth. I sleep higher once I don't overeat the closing meal of the day. You want to try this method, too!

Communication

I usually journey with an unlocked cellular phone, so every time I land someplace, I should buy a close-by SIM card to use and not put money into global roaming. In nowadays's traveling international, most subjects may be looked for your telephone, whether or not or now not bookings, bus/teach instances, Uber, recommendations, and so forth. Having a running cell cellphone with you will ensure you acquired't get lost. I furthermore can also carry out a little studies and download the most used apps for excursion on your excursion spot countries. When you've got were given your telephone and apps that the locals are acquainted with organized to go, you are already your own excursion manual.

Chapter 13: Debt Reduction Strategies

The Minimalist's Guide to Managing Debt

It is simple to turn out to be wealthy if you don't have any payments. I need to encompass debt discount strategies on this e-book due to the truth many people I apprehend don't have any debt and function made massive strides closer to their lengthy-time period monetary savings. You want to rapid end up rich in case you don't have automobile payments, scholar loans, credit score score rating gambling playing cards, scientific money owed, or maybe a mortgage. It takes some easy math and backbone. It's smooth to mention but very difficult to do, but it's even though possible.

The minimalist approach to life isn't pretty an lousy lot lowering bodily litter or major a greater spartan manner of life; it's additionally about developing financial peace and freedom. Managing and in the end disposing of debt is a essential detail of financial minimalism.

Managing debt thru a minimalist lens isn't just about paying off balances; it's approximately adopting a lifestyle and mind-set that prioritizes what without a doubt subjects. By simplifying your monetary life, that specialize in values, and adopting practical strategies, you could manage and do away with debt in a manner that brings economic peace and aligns collectively along with your desire for a miles much much less complicated life.

This minimalist technique to debt manipulate is not a brief restore; it's an prolonged-time period determination to dwelling with reason and making conscious monetary choices. It also can moreover require sacrifices and difficult choices, but the closing reward is financial freedom and the contentment of dwelling a existence unburdened thru debt and pointless complexity. It's approximately reclaiming manipulate of your monetary future and developing area for the opinions, relationships, and pastimes that bring proper fulfillment and delight.

Good Debts and Bad Debts

Good Debt, What Is It?

Any debt that would assist you grow your internet surely virtually really worth or produce future sales is right. Notably, it frequently has a low-interest price or annual percentage price (APR), usually less than 6%.

1.   Education: Taking on debt to pay for college is typically regarded as "right debt" because of the truth more training can increase your destiny profits, even though scholar loans can be a economic stress. Some people view pupil loans as an investment of their future because of this. Remember that for pupil mortgage debt to be deemed "appropriate," it have to satisfy those necessities: you must have carefully

taken into consideration low expenses of interest and the phrases of any scholar loans you are taking out.

2.   Property: A loan is a kind of financing used to buy actual property or a home. In the past, they have been one of the most steady types of debt due to their propensity for lower hobby expenses and potential to assist you in gathering fairness (contemplate grade by grade obtaining possession of your private home). Research before signing some factor, in particular a mortgage, as there is probably many transferring elements. For instance, you would in all likelihood pick among a difficult and fast-price and variable-charge loan. Essential change-offs exist amongst regular-charge and variable-fee mortgages; variable-charge mortgages are greater complicated and often have lower initial prices however bring the risk of fee hikes.

Bad Debt, What Is It?

Bad debt is credit taken out for charges that received't raise your internet without a doubt really worth or future earnings. Debt can also moreover additionally now and again be used to shop for devices that lose rate. Bad debt often includes a immoderate-interest charge at the time of buy or a variable fee that could increase at a excessive rate, this means that you'll likely wind up paying greater for gadgets that lose price over the years.

1. Credit playing gambling playing cards make (over)spending clean because swiping is psychologically masses less painful than delivering actual coins. However, the use of a credit score score card excessively can result in destiny issues. Credit gambling playing cards usually have immoderate APRs, every so often exceeding 20%, making reimbursement steeply-priced and including insult to harm. People commonly utilize credit score rating to buy devices like meals and garb, which they devour, in order that

they grow to be with little to not something to expose for that debt.

How can this sort of terrible debt be avoided? Create a technique for paying off your current credit score card debt, then use your credit card like a debit card. Use it quality for transactions you can complete with the finances in your economic group account. Making and sticking to a budget additionally let you keep your spending in take a look at, and aiming to build up an emergency fund same to three to six months' nicely well worth of charges can prevent you from the use of your credit score rating gambling cards whilst you do now not have cash.

1.   High-hobby loans with an hobby price or annual percentage price of 6% or extra are normally considered excessive-interest loans. They may additionally want to come inside the shape of personal loans or payday loans. These loans might be hard to pay off,

that could increase their rate as interest accrues and climbs.

These loans ought to most effective be utilized in emergencies after all the other options have been exhausted due to their immoderate-interest prices. It might be best to technique your debt similar to you address credit score rating card debt to save you relying on excessive-interest loans. Pay off any high-interest money owed and artwork toward installing location an emergency fund as fast as feasible to keep away from getting rid of new loans.

What about vehicle loans?

Car loans can be taken into consideration actual or horrible debt. Depending on several variables, along side your credit score score and the kind and size of the mortgage, some car loans may additionally additionally have high-interest prices, which can be horrible debt. On the alternative hand, a automobile can help you find out or hold a job, as a way to boom your earning ability. Therefore, an car loan also can be a satisfactory form of debt. If you're running in the path of disposing of exceptional money owed altogether, avoid shopping for new cars and go for a decent secondhand automobile that may do the equal pastime.

Strategies for Paying Off Debts

Understanding the scope of your debt is the first step in managing it. Create a easy evaluation of all your debts, which includes the amount owed, interest charges, and minimum payments. Seeing the whole lot in a single area facilitates make smooth what you're going through and lets in for a more streamlined approach. You have already discovered to determine what you really want and price and moreover reduce all over again on needless spending in Chapters 2 and 3. Taking these steps can loose up extra money to pay down debt.

The 2nd step is to create a easy debt compensation plan. Choose a debt compensation method that suits your situation and man or woman. Two commonplace techniques are the Debt Snowball (paying off smaller debts first) and the Debt Avalanche (paying off the exceptional hobby charges first). I use Debt Avalanche, so I don't accrue more debt with the immoderate-hobby costs. You must stay with one approach and make it a addiction.

The zero.33 step is to installation automatic payments to make certain you continuously pay on time. It takes the guesswork and emotion out of the method and helps keep away from overdue charges. Some places of work also can allow for deposits into distinct bank debts. I set up one bank account to pay bills ONLY and each other for non-bill costs. I prioritize bills, then economic economic financial savings, then precise stuff.

The fourth step is important: You need to determine to not taking over new debt as you determine on paying off modern-day-day balances. You ought to avoid credit score score card spending and different loans except crucial.

Debt Consolidation

Debt consolidation is a monetary technique combining severa money owed and obligations right into a single, greater doable mortgage. It is a device that might simplify debt compensation and, in some conditions, decrease the whole hobby load. It can also additionally moreover sound right at the start and may fit for you. However, you take out every other loan, which I don't advocate. It looks like a cop-out scenario for me and will maximum possibly no longer do you any top notch extended-time period. Remember, the goal is to construct appropriate spending behavior. If your debt feels overwhelming, don't hesitate to are searching for expert assist. A monetary counselor or advertising and marketing representative who knows your minimalist values can provide custom designed steering.

Building an Emergency Fund

Emergency price range are crucial to sound financial manipulate. An emergency fund gives a economic buffer for unexpected dreams like vehicle maintenance, clinical bills, or profits loss with out credit score gambling playing cards or loans. As a number one step closer to financial balance, creating this protection internet lets in you to deal with surprising prices without stressing and derailing your economic method.

Fund Size

First, decide your emergency fund duration. Common recommendation is to save 3 to six months of living fees. The quantity relies upon on your income stability and the amount of your commonplace spending. If you're starting to construct a fund, $500 to $1,000 should make a huge distinction.

Separate Account

Once you recognize your goal, open an emergency fund financial financial savings account. The emergency fund want to be separate from your checking or financial savings account to keep away from the use of it for non-emergencies. A no-fee account with easy get proper of access to will ensure you've got money even as wished.

Look at Your Current Budget

Setting a budget and reducing costs will assist you financial your emergency fund. Over time, tiny contributions add up. Consider automating the ones contributions to place a part of each paycheck into the emergency fund. Automation eliminates preference-making, making saving extra capability and constant.

Define What You Mean through Emergencies

Defining emergencies is crucial as you create your emergency fund. It will prevent you from spending the price variety on deliberate or non-pressing gadgets. Emergencies are sudden, urgent, and essential, like a giant car repair or health center bill. You'll most probable make use of the fund nicely if you explicitly outline its reason.

Track development

Building an emergency economic financial savings takes time in case you're beginning from scratch or living paycheck-to-paycheck. It also can include extraordinary sacrifices and a sturdy financial determination. Tracking your improvement and appreciating minor wins can encourage you. An emergency fund is a piece in development; adjust your emergency fund to healthy your dwelling expenses and budget as you change. If you need to make use of the fund, rebuild it proper now.

An emergency fund is essential to minimalist finance, reflecting readiness and conscientious dwelling. By building a monetary cushion, you can hobby on what topics and keep away from the anxiety of residing on the edge. Building and preserving an emergency fund calls for financial honesty and recognition. It's a practical method to dwelling and embraces a philosophy that values stability, intentionality, and the freedom to cope with lifestyles's united statesand downs with self guarantee and peace of thoughts. Emergency price range are a clean but powerful tool that might beautify your economic properly-being and high-quality of life, whether or no longer starting to construct your economic basis or strengthening it.

Chapter 14: Continuing Education

Financial Education Is Ongoing and Can Improve Your Financial Decisions

To enhance your financial talents, actively pursue education:

Read: Start with economic books, articles, blogs, and research papers. Everyone can find out records, from beginners to specialists. Books and net sites written through using economic specialists can offer precious insights and techniques.

Attend finance workshops and seminars: Many businesses and faculties offer severa workshops and seminars, from budgeting to complex making an funding techniques. These workshops allow palms-on experience, questions, and networking with like-minded people. A financial advertising and marketing consultant can offer individualized steering on your particular monetary role. These professionals can verify your price variety, set potential goals, and devise a plan. Make pleasant your guide is licensed and extraordinary.

Take on-line guides and webinars: The internet has made education more available. Online structures provide private finance and investment education. These courses whether or no longer or not unfastened or paid are designed for novices via superior levels. The on line gear allow self-paced studying.

Join economic groups: Peer learning is probably beneficial. Participate in monetary boards and companies with like-minded human beings. Ask questions, observe from others, and percentage your insights.

Stay up to date: The economic global is dynamic, so keep up with dispositions, information, and prison pointers. Stay current-day-day with economic information and join in applicable newsletters.

Practice and placed into impact: Lastly, reading, workshops, and session show beneficial nice at the same time as carried out. Start the use of what you take a look at and adjust as you realize greater.

You will gain the competencies and facts to with a bit of luck navigate the economic worldwide via the usage of using reading, taking publications, consulting with professionals, and using on-line resources. This region of gaining knowledge of improves your financial nicely-being. It lets you make strategic decisions that reflect your values and aspirations. Maintain your hobby and revel in of thought via surrounding yourself with minimalist inspirations.

Chapter 15: Embrace Contentment

Minimalism is gaining popularity as a way of delight and fulfillment for an increasing number of individuals. The minimalist way of existence questions our dependency on possessions and their consolation. Remember that minimalism's primary desires are pleasure and brilliant in place of quantity.

Redefining Success

Success and happiness correlate to more stuff, cash, and reward in a consumer-pushed world. You shall redefine success as taking component in what you have. It will teach you that actual contentment comes from valuing what's essential, not gathering possessions.

Prioritizing Interactions and Experiences

Adopting a minimalist lifestyle permits you to vicinity more value on interpersonal interactions, tremendous reviews, and individual development. Quality time with circle of relatives, interests, and enjoyable sports activities takes priority. Such vast interactions regularly improve happiness and a sense of reason.

It's better to have fewer superb gadgets than many low-fine devices

The minimalist philosophy prioritizes excellence above extra in all endeavors. You fill your lives with subjects and those that keep in mind to you via the relationships you domesticate and the connections you keep. Placing a trouble on first-class lets in to clean the intellectual and emotional litter that most possibly can disrupt your every day existence.

Meditation and Personal Development

Minimalism is a way of life that demanding situations you to prioritize what in fact topics. You will observe what brings you the most pleasure and happiness thru introspection and improvement. This introspection can pave the way to profound realizations and a truly reflective existence.

Positive Environmental and Monetary Effects

In most times, prioritizing first rate over amount makes more revel in economically and ecologically. Spend your coins on durable items to reduce environmental impact and sell ethical shopping for selections. You will locate monetary peace of thoughts with the aid of simply residing inner your method.

Try Not to Compare

The key to finding your way is to keep away from assessment the least bit costs. Discontentment brought on with the beneficial useful resource of evaluation frequently results in moves that contradict your values. Your individuality, dreams, and aspirations can be valid thru staying on direction. Rather than specializing in maintaining up with fantastic human beings, this approach encourages introspective growth and success. Finding happiness and making options actual to who you are and what you need is feasible even as you take delivery of your adventure without assessment.

Rejoice in Advancement

Shift your recognition from cloth acquisition to accountable economic increase. In pursuing monetary independence, it's critical to apprehend and honor even the smallest achievements. The minimalist way of life emphasizes steady introspection and planned movement. Make fine you're nevertheless at the proper track together together with your monetary desires via often reviewing your prices, debt payments, and preferred economic condition.

Chapter 16: A Whole New World

Reflection at the Long-time period Potential of Financial Minimalism

Living with as little coins as viable is gaining reputation in this day of brilliant materialism. The number one dreams of financial minimalism are to live inner or beneath one's approach, to reduce pointless spending, and to prioritize economic goals that uphold one's ideals and life imaginative and prescient. Opportunities for this long-time period economic plan replicate shifts in how people typically think about what it method to be rich, satisfied, and a achievement.

Freedom From Monetary Burdens and Control Over Your Own Life

Taking control of your monetary future is interior benefit with the assist of the minimalist approach to personal finance. You can lessen debt and economic strain with the useful resource of carefully thinking about your spending and saving conduct. This try might also will let you retire early, pursue your passions, or take extended trips down the road to retirement. Simplifying your charge range additionally assist you to stay a far much less worrying and additional pleasant existence with the resource of making a living an enabler as opposed to a burden.

Ethical and Long-time period Consumption

Minimalism to your financial lifestyles regularly coexists with a heightened focus of your ecological footprint. Placing a higher precedence on reviews in place of material possessions and on top notch rather than quantity encourages a more moral and sustainable manner of shopping. The shift in consumer conduct may also moreover push corporations to create environmentally pleasant merchandise and adopt greater sustainable practices, developing a virtuous cycle of character ethics and business enterprise duty.

The Rise of the Gig Economy and the New Economic Order

In a worldwide wherein traditional system protection is declining, simplifying your monetary scenario also can provide peace of thoughts. This, in flip, allows you to with any luck address assignment adjustments, freelance, or start your personal enterprise enterprise with the aid of encouraging residing beneath your approach and saving for unexpected wishes. Since the gig economic machine is most often quick and bendy, this form of employee is more likely to be financially clever and able to handling unpredictable earnings streams. Minimalism in personal finance gives techniques for coping with the modern financial weather.

The State of Your Mind and Body, in General

Spending accurately and living through way of the use of your values are two strategies to enhance your exceptional of life and decrease pressure Financial minimalism objectives that will help you cognizance on the things that depend maximum to you financially It furthermore encourages you to fee studies, relationships, and person development over fabric possessions, which may additionally advantage your prolonged-term nicely-being.

In the long term, the advantages of financial minimalism amplify a long manner past person charge variety. Its concepts align with societal shifts prioritizing environmental consciousness, personal flourishing, and monetary adaptability. More and further people adopting this outlook have the potential to seriously adjust buying behavior, organization techniques, and individual happiness. The thoughts of economic minimalism will permit you to gain extra happiness and stability.

Chapter 17: How To Save Cash On Clothes

Ok, welcome to the phase teaching you a way to shop cash on garments. Although there are such loads of hints and recommendations, there may be one that reins mainly others! Here is the maximum important step with the intention to maintain the maximum coins lengthy-time period: increase your personal fashion!

By developing your non-public fashion, you no longer nice appearance GOOD in clothes that match your particular man or woman and luxury stage, but you furthermore might keep away from speedy-fashion trends.

Fast fashion dispositions are THE WORST!

Not pleasant do they motive waste to the planet, however in addition they cause leaks in your budget. If you're constantly looking for the "what's in style," you're constantly shopping for and looking for your way into society's useless expectations.

Developing your very personal style! Seek garments that look real on YOUR frame. Find garments which might be comfortable in YOUR frame. Stop believing that the entirety on the mannequins or marketed to you on the telephone is a MUST HAVE.

By growing your non-public fashion, you'll save you comparing yourself to wonderful human beings and stop normally attempting to shop for your way into a few exclusive lifestyles.

I mean, come on! Americans play the silliest coins video games.

It's time to miss about how Mr. Jones prioritizes his price variety.

We can forestall searching for into the game!

Yes, we're actual friends, but we also do what is amazing for our lives. Honestly, that is opting out of hours and hours walking for a purposeless imaginative and prescient to buy topics that we don't want. And virtually, most customarily it brings us muddle in place of joy.

Let's be accomplished! I imply, it's far 2023. We can't have sufficient cash to play the Jones game anymore!

We're using the rollercoaster of 40-12 months immoderate inflation and it is reducing away at our gasoline and meals budgets. Like insanely! Things need to change.

It's proper sufficient to quickly allow flow of strategies life changed into to revel in life now the brilliant we're able to. And that's by using manner of the use of ditching the cash video games.

In this e-book, we'll deliver out all the first-class recommendations and guidelines we've used to preserve our own family clothed.

Start studying what patterns artwork fine together with your frame these days. Not your body "at the equal time as." Your body in recent times!

No rely variety wherein you determined you have to be with regards to weight, you have to enjoy extremely good on your present day country now.

So begin figuring out what clothes look superb for your. Not clothes you recognize but virtually do now not paintings together with your form.

Companies undergo super lengths to increase "brands." Start growing your personal logo with the beneficial resource of tailoring your personal style.

I understand developing your very personal private style could not appear like some thing that would mechanically prevent money, however it does help us begin turning into intentional with our apparel alternatives.

At the instant, advertising and advertising and advertising has clothes everywhere! When we enjoy blue, on-line purchasing is there any time of day. Super clearance markdown offers pop up in our feeds, growing countless streams of "gives too nicely to bypass up."

Developing a fashion helps slender the powerful advertising and advertising.

Clothes can resultseasily turn out to be a way to unload cash. It's the exceptional treatment for such a lot of feelings and number one-international-problems.

Feeling insecure after a split? You're one buying spree a ways from a current-day existence (or at least that's what the films teach us).

Excited for that upcoming experience? Why now not store for a brand new beach fabric wardrobe?

And clothes are lovely! A new outfit can decorate the mood. However, it is able to get EXPENSIVE! Especially even as buying retail. Here is every specific little bit of first advice: don't maintain retail. Like ever.

The best time I've offered retail is because of the truth I desired a selected piece of garb that I may additionally additionally or might not have located via thrifting. For my first public speakme gig, I did purchase a blazer retail.

Anything aside from that, I'm shopping for clearance, or better yet THRIFT!

Thrifting subjects a lot. Not simplest do you lessen the waste within the international and shop money, however the thrift shops often assist impactful charities. Many thrift shops act because the coins cow for endeavors that help our society.

For example, there is one thrift preserve in my town whose proceeds go to fund a big network lawn. The nutritious food that's grown is allotted via their soup kitchen and meals pantry. So now not best am I saving coins via shopping for 2nd-hand, however the coins I do spend goes to assist those in need in my community.

For actual! I apprehend many human beings have a trouble toward shopping for thrift however considering all of the proper it does - saving coins, decreasing landfills, and helping others - I noticeably recommend giving it a try!

Yes, you do should look ahead to stains, holes, or missing buttons, however the offers you find out are nicely well well worth the hazard.

Capsule dresser

One way to hold cash on garments is to buy a few intentional portions that artwork together. For example, if you have three shirts, three pants, and 3 jackets in a color scheme that works collectively, you have got efficaciously 27 high-quality garments you could placed on. By retaining portions in colors that look top together, you don't want to fear approximately any mismatching!

Not most effective is that this an super minimalism knowledge, however it's also a competencies to preserve cash because you forestall looking one million new clothes to get a million new looks.

A fundamental pill fabric cloth cabinet need to include the following:

A undying coat

Button up shirt

T-shirts

Nice pant healthy

Jeans

Simple get dressed

Etc

If the colours of all above work collectively - no clashing - you have got severa splendid combos that paintings for masses of activities or conditions. And with the aid of manner of using purchasing for genuinely one or jackets that artwork nicely with the whole thing, you don't should preserve spending coins searching for an appropriate jacket of the week!

And none of this wants to be high-dollar. You can thrift lots of these. Because it's miles a pill cloth cloth wardrobe, entire of timeless devices, you shop cash and skip the short style frenzy that collects on our credit playing cards.

Of course, you don't ought to be so minimalistic that you first-rate permit 5 articles of garb. But via incorporating well-picked portions that paintings together, you could advantage such a whole lot of appears with out the need for filling the closet.

Hand-Me-Downs

You understand how people say "we need extra love inside the global?" I don't understand if they say that, however that looks like some component we want to say.

Want to recognize what's a excellent gesture of affection? Gifting your clothes to someone who goals them.

This is the truest in phrases of kids. Children need clothes and even though some garments may be less highly-priced, the adventure of apparel isn't always. Having to buy the whole lot yet again each length exchange honestly affords up.

It takes lots of clothes to hold a infant protected and heat from starting to commencement.

So many wonderful sizes. So many precise seasons. So a good deal money!

This is why hand-me-downs are golden!

When I was a child, I changed into raised with the useful resource of a single mother for many years. But we have been blessed!

In our church have been multiple sisters barely older than me with the same body-type. Their father come to be a scientific expert and generous with their abundance.

There is probably instances wherein I'd be capable of go to their residence and they could find out garments that now not in shape them but seemed incredible on me!

High exceptional, fashionable clothes we'd by no means be able to find out the cash for on my circle of relatives's finances. I'd walk far from their bed room with trash baggage whole of wardrobes I modified into proud to put on even in middle faculty. I'll all the time be pleased about that circle of relatives!

There's beauty in hand-me-downs too. Every once in a while, I'll see an outfit my infant outgrew donned with the useful aid of a friend's littler one. Oh the pleasure it brings to look that equal outfit once more getting the locate it impossible to resist merits!

If you don't like hand-me-downs because of a few shape of stigma, revel in loose to drop it!

It doesn't make feel to anticipate simplest horrific humans use hand-me-downs. That type of coins will maintain you spending manner more for a societal contemporary that doesn't make revel in.

Will there be stains? Yes. Will there be holes? Probably. Do you have to dress your toddler up within the ones garments for photo day? Absolutely no longer!

Chapter 18: Feel Unfastened To Request Clothes

There's a girl at my church, Lauren, who has the same frame type as mine the exceptional thing? She has a super fashion enjoy!

So in the future I asked her if I should get preserve of her unwanted clothes. Like in place of dropping them off at Goodwill or a few other second-hand preserve, have to shed donate them to me first? And she did!

I honestly have such a whole lot of clothes from her that I certainly love! I wager this whole detail is that hand-me-downs don't have to cease at maturity.

And you may ask someone for their hand-me-downs.

It might likely appear bizarre, however whilst you think about it, why is it? Because we don't want them to count on we're lousy?

Ah, see…

That's the Jones recreation costing us cash and we're finished with that!

To be honest, my husband and I aren't even hurting for coins. There had been years of penny-pinching to get via way of, however that grow to be right sufficient.

But even now that we are snug and can find out the cash for brand spanking new garments, we however buy 2d-hand. Or ask stylish human beings throughout the equal duration for his or her hand-me-downs.

Why?

Because it is a more inexperienced machine on all fronts.

I keep coins.

I lessen apparel waste.

I boom a style that may be a clean combination of mine and whoever's I'm inheriting.

So yeah, I pays retail prices for gadgets, but if I see Lauren continuously searching proper in my period, I'm gonna ask for her hand-me-downs.

Not in a needy kind of manner. But truly due to the truth I apprehend humans drop off to Goodwill. Why now not inherit it first, respiration existence into friendships and patterns?

Husband: After seeing Rachel do this and get a few sweet clothes I decided to do the same thing with a few people from paintings. Believe it or not, I get a number of the biggest compliments from clothes I haven't offered. Thanks Jennifer, Landon, and Paul.

Thrift

Yeah, we knew this changed into coming as a section in itself. Thrift! I truely love thrifting. Honestly, I likely purchase 2 or three contemporary objects a yr. Usually I purchase a move well with (outstanding love my American Flag 2-piece I positioned on amazon!), some merch from church to help close by venture journeys, and miscellaneous gadgets much like the blazer for my first talking occasion.

But otherwise, once I'm now not bumming off human beings for his or her garments (hahaha), I keep secondhand.

When I have come to be 8 or 9 years vintage, my mom flew me to see my Nana at the same time as she changed into living in California. During the ones unmarried-mom years and in advance than my Nana moved in with us, I'd spend a bit of time at some degree within the summer season at their residence in Sacramento. My nana may also want to take me to buy new garments, however in vicinity of spending gobs of money, she'd take me to the thrift shop to shop for second-hand clothes. I cherished locating all of the funky patterns from the West coast that weren't frequently determined in my Texas thrift shops.

Now whenever we excursion, if we've got a 2d to save like each ordinary tour past time, we are capable of are searching out a second-hand keep! Instead of purchasing at retail shops, we browse close by 2nd-hand shops. You although get a strong vibe of the place based totally mostly on gadgets located and come home with exceptional souvenirs.

Plus you spend a fraction of the rate

In 2021, my own family and I deliberate a huge adventure out West! The plan turned into we might fly into Arizona, lease a car, and adventure over to the San Diego vicinity, as a lot as Sacramento, over to Yellowstone, then south decrease lower back to Arizona. Because this became a largely camping adventure with only some Airbnb's and resorts along the way, we wanted additives.

First save you, Goodwill.

We have been capable of select out up clothes, blankets, books, and cookware that we'd want for the ride. Honestly, I located my desired math hoodie at that Goodwill.

The essential thrift save names humans apprehend are Goodwill and Salvation military which might be every nicely stores. However, there can be one-of-a-kind second-hand stores that honestly act because the coins cow for fantastic reasons!

I'll supply examples.

One second-hand preserve in town generates cash that finances a garden and soup kitchen, serving loads of hungry within the community.

I used to devour at this soup kitchen each day they have been open even as in university to keep coins. I developed many friendships and won masses perception from actually being attentive to unique humans's tales and getting to know them over lunch.

By shopping for garments, home decor, books, and one of a kind objects used at this thrift save, I not best preserve cash but moreover fund a few factor that blesses others? Yeah, I'm thrifting!

Another 2d-hand shop on the town generates cash to manual nonprofits housing girls coming out of abusive conditions. All of those shops run the equal. They take in donations from the community, sell another time to the community, after which use those finances to help inclined people of our community!

All at the same time as saving you cash.

"Well, it's difficult to find out matters in fashion." Life is much less complicated while we allow circulate of what's "in-style" and normally are trying to find the following fashion.

That is why developing your very very personal private fashion is so essential.

For instance, ever for the reason that starting my social media@RachelandTheRiveters, I've found out that the iconic "Rosie" look is amusing to shop for.

If Rosie the Riveter became a doll, what might she placed on? That is now how I keep.

I've been leaning towards patriotic patterns or shades which consist of pink, white, and blue. Ever because of the fact coming across this concern be counted, it is been a whole lot much less complex for me to hold and dress. Once I decided a "appearance," shopping for have turn out to be more fun!

Now once I keep second-hand, I browse the aisles searching out a few difficulty pink, white, and blue. Obviously, I put on distinctive topics, too. But having a "fashion" makes the revel in greater streamlined and amusing! Like my very personal patriotic garb scavenger hunt.

To be honest, I'm at the hunt for such a American flag fits. I know Amazon and different retailers have sold many. I see images of people sporting them all the time! So now I just lay in wait till one among them shows up at my community 2d-hand shop. I can't deliver myself to buy one at retail, but as quick as I spot one 2d-hand, it's mine!

Then there are ethical motives to store 2nd hand. Let's communicate approximately the consequences of "rapid fashion" or constantly retaining up with the trends.

Did you recognize that the commonplace US customer throws away 80 one.5lbs of clothes each three hundred and sixty five days? Like, genuinely one person!

We purchase and donate. Some gets offered at 2nd-hand shops, however plenty of it is going to landfills or is burned.

By searching out second-hand, you save you garb waste! All while saving cash!

Chapter 19: Identify Manufacturers You Need Excessive Excellent

Now, I'm not saying that 2nd-hand buying is all peaches and roses (or however the pronouncing is going). There are downsides. Sometimes you'll fall in love with a bit of garb you determined IN YOUR SIZE EVEN (looking at you, Goodwill - why y'all were given to prioritize color coding instead of sizes besides?), best to find out that same piece of garb has a button lacking. Or a stain Or the garb modified into glaringly nicely-loved because of the reality the material has been worn down through friction extra time to end up less thick and extra see-via. Think inner thighs on leggings and over-stretched chests on shirts.

That is why I encourage you to begin figuring out producers you want and deem awesome. For me, I love locating a terrific banana republic. For my husband, I assume he appears terrific in Express clothes. Now, none of these are pretty bougie, however I definitely wouldn't be capable of pay retail for the ones equal clothes in their shops of starting area.

By figuring out clothing manufacturers you want and characteristic witnessed hold up nicely, you're quicker to make picks on garb in the store. I don't have a list of "great clothing manufacturers to appearance out for" aside from my favorites together with Banana Republic or call brands at the side of Vera Wang. If there's ever a amazing apparel line advertised to you continuously through social media (because of the fact the set of rules is conscious what you want through now), take a look at it and don't forget that call on the same time as searching through the aisles at the equal time as thrifting.

Shop Off Season

I love buying at resale stores for my youngsters's garments. There's shops in which you could sell your vintage clothes and buy new-to-you objects. I love those shops!

Often, they have got clearance instances. This is usually how they'll be looking for to promote off summer time devices from their cabinets after the season inside the fall or while they are trying to sell off winter stuff as the time rolls to summer season. This is at the same time as you buy! During the off-season!

Once expenses are marked down, you pass in and also you pick out or have your infant pick out out their cloth cupboard for the subsequent one year. Be high-quality to be aware of sizes on the same time as they may be toddlers due to the reality you'll want to assume what length they'll be in what season. If your children are older, have them pick out out out out their subsequent twelve months's clothing.

Wash Less Often

One fantastically way to maintain coins on clothes is to wash them a notable deal a great deal much less regularly.

Time out: to be honest, I by no means concept I'd be a hippie, however right proper here we're. But a number of their practices make experience!

How regularly are you rolling down hills within the grass? Like, realistically? How approximately splashing in puddles? When emerge as the last epic meals fight you were in?

Currently, maximum humans are silly and don't stay like that (me covered, so don't anticipate I'm seeking to rat every person out). And however, we wash our garments after every wear as despite the fact that we do stay like that.

But then there's the chair.

Oh, positive, there may be the cherished chair. You recognize, the chair for your bed room that doesn't do a good buy apart from stack clothes too worn to be hung once more up however too clean to retire to the hamper.

Embrace the chair!

Because the chair is the situation our clothes can continue to be in maximum of the time if we're organized to break out the trap of doing laundry as frequently as we've got were given.

And that is thru really washing tons less.

But with the intention to wash lots much less, we need to preserve our garments in a country that we're capable of wash masses less.

Now, in case you do roll down hills, bounce in puddles, and get into meals fights - by means of way of all manner flow into! Don't permit the fear of washing garments too often save you you!

However, in case you aren't, and your clothes are not dirty or stinky, keep them in this type of manner that they may be capable of air out.

This is the most crucial step of washing much less. Any moisture that receives piled below numerous clothing has the capability to interrupt the complete stack.

So perhaps not stack barely damp clothes one after the other on the chair.

If you do have region, undergo in thoughts setting up worn however but clean clothes to air out. This received't paintings if you have a jam-packed closet and it can't air out, main to that subtle but unsightly mould fragrance.

By washing lots less regularly, you moreover may also prolong the fibers of your garb over the years. Each wash makes use of friction to smooth our garments, however this identical friction deteriorates the energy of the fibers through the years. Not to say the damage due to excessive heat of the dryers.

Lessen the quantity of damage on your clothes, therefore prolonging their use, resulting in much less need to buy new garments. All thru washing them a whole lot less often!

But nicely wash them much less. We in no way need to be gross most effective for the sake of saving a few bucks. If they gross, they gross. I guess the rule of thumb of thumb is probably to wash as wanted. Put a glowing outfit on that day but have been given in a meals fight? Feel free to wash that when the only put on!

If its gross, its gross. If its decently easy, preserve it as lots as air out for the subsequent positioned on.

Husband right here: Don't try this your underwear. Give them regular washes. If you are a man, I understand you are getting your moneys properly well really worth out of them besides sporting them till they basically fall apart. Also…. If you could fragrance yourself, others can heady scent you hundreds more.

Line Dry Clothes

You realize what feels so "Little House on the prairie" but in an terrific way? Line-drying garments!

I recognize we've already said this in a few special ebook Frugal Living for Parents: How to Save Money on Housing, Utilities, and Transportation but it is nicely sincerely really worth citing once more!

Line drying clothes looks like it'd be a pain, but it is the maximum zen approach of managing laundry!

There's not some thing extra poetically lovely than your whity tighties swaying inside the wind. For real! It's so captivating.

It's not a signal of poverty to look strings of outfits solar bleaching within the outside, or off the patio, or amongst homes.

It's a sign of self-sustainability. It's a sign of domestic tranquility.

And it saves money! Not best on heating the dryer, having the dryer warm temperature up your own home inside the summer time months after which having to pay greater for AC to run the dryer.

It furthermore prolongs the sturdiness of your garments.

This is the identical principle for laundry an awful lot less. Use your dryer tons much less to reduce the quantity of heavy friction and excessive warmth to the fibers of your chosen clothes which you need to remaining!

Plus the youngsters will love playing cowl and are looking for for amid the swaying bedsheets. Their creativeness prospers and the garments dry! Win Win!

Use Less Detergent

Do you understand what America is addicted to? Using too much detergent!

Yes, the Tide pods are appropriate due to the reality they'll be in my view packaged. It's now not tough to realize the amount to throw in. Not for intake via! Still no longer sure why that changed into ever a problem.

Overall, we use an excessive amount of laundry detergent.

Believe it or not, for high-performance washers, you could use teaspoons of liquid detergent or tablespoons of powdered detergent. For a pinnacle loader, you could get with the beneficial resource of using tablespoons of liquid detergent or four tablespoons of powder.

But Rachel, aren't your clothes gross? No! Not in any respect! In reality, the usage of an excessive amount of detergent, counter-intuitively, have to make your clothes greater gross!

See, excessive detergent can't wash out well after which leaves a residue. This residue permeates garments, preventing them from washing absolutely smooth. It moreover leaves a residue interior your washing gadget, main to high priced maintenance or maybe premature gadget alternative.

But why need to the laundry detergent caps have those markers?

Now, I'm really now not this form of conspiracy theorists who believes each company is out to get us. But it's miles going without announcing that businesses are out for earnings. And they make extra profits in case you use more detergent with every load, therefore buying greater frequently.

If you are inside the dependancy of the usage of the overall cap, attempt certainly really fizzling out a chunk. Experiment with each load. Unless the garments undergo heavy soilage from artwork or whatnot (or those meals fights we said in advance), you probable don't need that a good buy.

Even a mild washing in warmness water will do the trick. However, we use only a small squirt of liquid detergent in cold water and function in no way had really anyone bitch approximately a stench. And we offer hugs all the time!

Either our garments have end up clean the use of less detergent, or the friends we hug are too scared to say something. I'm quite nice our garments simply get clean using masses less detergent.

Buy One Kind of Sock

One of my least desired chores (2nd to sweeping/vacuuming) is laundry - no matter the fact that line drying does make the complete technique a miles better revel in.

However, the worst a part of laundry for me in my view ought to be the socks. Matching socks is the most drudgery existence can ever provide. And I'm sick of it. So lots just so we embraced The Hub's concept: purchase most effective one form of sock.

Not first-rate does searching for one shape of sock remove the time spent matching forever and ever, however it receives rid of waste from throwing away people with misplaced suits. It additionally prevents you from falling into the lure of "oh, study the ones adorable socks."

Toe socks, amusing socks, loopy socks. All long gone!

But Rachel, doesn't that suck all the pride from your life?

Not in any respect! In reality, it added pleasure to my existence! I've reduce my time spent sock matching exponentially. When we are on foot low because of the truth we turn out to be lacking a few, as notoriously takes area, we sincerely purchase more of the equal a lot much less steeply-priced type.

Yes, there are a few a laugh socks that I do love but not unusual, I'm conforming to the black anklet all of the time. Bonus elements because of the truth The Hubs and I positioned on the equal size, further disposing of the want to buy particular kinds and type remarkable youngsters.

Disclaimer: I furthermore preserve some wool socks. This allows me keep money through the use of decreasing our house's heating. Never regulate the thermostat in winter in case you're barefoot. Put on some thick wool socks first and notice the distinction it makes!

Avoid Sales When You Don't Need Anything

One of my favourite memes is the complete "you save a hundred% through not looking for what you don't need."

I've fallen for this dozens of instances. You see a few factor you shape of like, understand it's miles on sale, after which purchase it right now as it's this sort of "good deal."

But it isn't a good deal if you don't use it, or if that money may be higher spent somewhere else together with tackling credit score rating score card debt.

Now, in case you are attempting to find a specific object after which it occurs to be on sale: winner winner chook dinner! Take the blessing!

But don't in truth take a luke-warm temperature object to the cart as it's on sale. That's now not a good buy. That's the shop dumping devices they don't want into your closet in which you don't need it every.

Repurpose Old Clothing

When I grow to be in immoderate university (thankfully earlier than the age of smartphones and your boredom delivered about advent), I commenced crafting shirts with the beneficial useful resource of protection-pinning scarves collectively over a tank top. It have emerge as so clean, so adorable, and brought about such a number of compliments!

As time went on, I picked up stitching on a machine. I'd craft handbags and awesome random subjects. My mom have become a huge fan of suggests like "America's Next Top Model." Watching on the aspect of her gave me concept to attempt my hand at crafting garments.

Although I in no way grew into a professional seamstress or style designer, I did have fun turning antique garments into new clothes.

If you also are foxy and characteristic time for your arms for creativity (really, we have to all make time for extra creativity), take a few different take a look at your donation bag and spot if there's any belief.

Now, there may be the trap of "Oh, I may also moreover need to..." after which the bag remains for each other three hundred and sixty five days because it's every other undertaking piled up on duties. That's not useful.

However, if it's far realistic at the way to redecorate some clothes for an a great deal less high-priced material cupboard exchange, then sure!

Also, don't allow a hollow or tear for your preferred outfit make you finish the reference to that outfit.

In all honesty, with rapid style how it's far, it would sense like a higher deal to simply pass buy each exclusive ten-dollar t-blouse than repair a hole in yours. However, the time and love this is going into mending a favorite piece of clothing reinforces that love for the clothing.

Not only that, however it reduces the demand for additonal "rapid style." The extra we location fee on what we have already got rather than looking for every other "brilliant deal," the higher our monetary institution balances and the arena becomes!

Even shopping for 2d-hand clothes and revamping them is a terrific opportunity! Just don't buy garments too huge on the way to use as extra fabric. Please go away the larger sizes for individuals who want them. It'd be terrible to have to shop for second-hand because of the truth that's all your finances permits great to discover your length notoriously now not available.

We need to be thoughtful of others!

Household

Now that we've had been given garments blanketed, let's head into circle of relatives items financial financial savings!

Get a membership

For some of us, getting a club membership to a bulk store like Sam's or Costco truely makes experience. Yeah, there may be the charge as quickly as a 365 days, however past that, it's miles financial financial savings.

Their rotisserie chickens are massive but the same fee as subject stores. Their bulk is higher. Their generics are higher! That is, if you may purchase it and keep it (together with food storage it truely is in particular critical to have - don't skimp out on it.)

In truth, frugal residing pause: permit's speak approximately food garage.

Yeah, this likely suits higher inside the beginning of the gathering for the duration of groceries, however the problem ought to be pointed out often.

Most human beings are one paycheck or far from going in the crimson.

What if there is a activity loss? No, I'm no longer proper right here to freak you out. But I am proper here to place down some realistic scenarios and communicate approximately how food storage cushions those capability economic blows.

By having food garage, it truly is actually extra meals saved away for use later, you're able to take care of losing the technique because you recognize your circle of relatives will no matter the truth that consume.

But it isn't just method losses that food storage permits with!

Imagine a heavy typhoon leaving you snowed in for days without strong get right of access to to the shop. The shipping trucks being not able to get to the shop to reshelve food.

Your food garage continues your own family fed and warm inner!

Where is the notable region to bulk up your food garage? At the massive golf equipment (hi there, we did make it complete circle!)

If you are in a smaller vicinity, it may be properly nicely worth skipping the huge club shops simply due to the reality they do are available in bulk which takes up extent.

It's now not well surely really worth looking for pallets of objects because it's a higher deal if it approach you'll be crowded indoors your living vicinity.

Remember, living regions are for residing - now not storage. However, vital food garage may be stored in precise locations with a chunk creativity.

For instance, one time we went beneath settlement for a domestic and I even have become so excited that I started packing right now! However, the deal fell thru on the final minute and it come to be such an emotionally devastating blow that I didn't have the want to unpack the whole thing all over again. So, I clearly positioned a tablecloth over the pinnacle of my containers and made it into a piece of faux furnishings.

Even although the objects packed away weren't meals (it changed into really muddle I held until I began perfecting the artwork of letting stuff move), the equal technique may be used to hold meals garage.

You can placed meals storage in flat totes and store under the mattress. No concerns about bugs or rodents in case you keep it in a food safe tote.

Seriously, having a few food handy in case of some trouble occurs is genuinely clever.

Gah, I need to get off this food storage kick.

Okay, again to getting a club. If there are gadgets you purchase some of and frequently, a club club may be proper for you and your own family.

Plus the shopping for enjoy is a laugh! You're capable of store, try samples (thank goodness strict covid policies are over - knock on wooden), or maybe get a decently priced dinner as a praise at their cafe. Yeah, it is no longer the maximum wholesome desire, but it's although top notch to experience an outsized slice of pizza every every so often.

Husband proper proper right here: Even if you don't have a massive own family and don't want to buy bulk, there are such lots of different benefits from having a membership. You can get reductions on vehicle leases and special offerings, get a percent lower again from every buy (2% on most purchases), and get fuel for inexpensive. Sam's Club offers unfastened transport on most devices and free curbside pickup with their Plus club. Plus, we will prevent in there and get a warm dog blend for $1.38. The personal label manufacturers, Member's Mark for Sam's Club and Kirkland

Signature for Costco (Sorry BJ's I don't realise what your emblem is), genuinely do stack as much as the "National Brands". Trust me once I tell you that those companies have personnel dedicated to creating the ones merchandise as accurate as, or better, than the ones country wide manufacturers. And if you simply don't like a few issue, they typically have amazing circulate decrease returned suggestions – No chance, all reward.

Buy in bulk

If you've had been given the distance for domestic garage, a manner to shop cash can be trying to find in bulk. You should buy masses of factors in bulk from meals, diapers, lavatory paper, and plenty of others. By searching for in bulk, you are lowering the want for packaging and therefore cast off greater waste too.

However, if you've have been given a small vicinity, there is handiest hundreds bulk shopping for you could do for my part. If you've had been given near own family or pals, endure in mind attempting to find in bulk together and simply taking what you need to hold in your own home whilst the opportunity activities take what they need for his or her house.

If you are in a small studio, it may now not make revel in to make investments in the Sam's Club membership. However, if you've had been given a huge circle of relatives with many wants, buying in bulk will be a very good investment.

There are cons to looking for in bulk. One is that you is probably tempted to overuse. If you've were given one thousand paper towel rolls spherical, you are much more likely to apply way more than you need definitely due to the reality it's far there. Although the charge in step with unit for getting in bulk is much less costly, in case you use increasingly of the product virtually because it feels extensive in your private home, it won't be less highly-priced.

Also, searching for meals in bulk might also additionally bring about spoilage if now not used brief or preserved. Buying food in bulk is high-quality for canning and freezing. However, if you aren't there but, that is right enough Just purchase what you will devour without bulk buying topics a very good way to waste.

Chapter 20: Borrow Items

This one isn't my desired due to the fact in truth as an introvert; it feels much less complex to avoid people. BUT in case you want one particular pastime completed with a specific tool and can avoid spending a ton of cash by way of way of borrowing stated device from a pal or family member, it's miles a higher deal.

We in no manner need to be this form of individuals who borrows some factor and then in no way remembers to return it.

Oh, it is the equal feeling of debt however in location of agency debt from banks like loans it's non-public.

We have a excellent manner to head back them inside a well timed way otherwise it isn't a bargain as it expenses us some dating overseas cash.

They is probably disappointed with us or indignant, or on every occasion you look at them you sting realizing you preserve forgetting to move returned that problem. Or worse - you completely forget approximately the complete association and the factor is in reality sitting in your private home such as you've had it all of the time. However, they remember and silently steam interior on every occasion they're spherical you. But then you certainly absolutely surely assume they will be getting extra crabbed in age however virtually, it is because of the fact you FORGOT TO RETURN THE THING?!

See, this is why this isn't my preferred, but if you can actually borrow the item, do the interest without procrastination, then go again the issue within the proper quantity of time, then do that as it saves lots money!

Especially if it's far a energy tool sort of object which you want for one clean project.

Bonus factors if it's far a neighbor. Then you build that sense of network we regularly lack.

Rent Tools

If you don't have everyone community to borrow from, keep in mind renting those equipment you simplest want as soon as in region of often.

Now, if it's miles a tool this is used frequently or you operate it for paintings, purchasing for your very non-public is an investment. However, if you are simply needing it one time for a one-shot task, renting is probably the maximum frugal approach.

Be positive to test fees. Shopping spherical helps make certain you're spending the least quantity for a mission nicely performed!

Simplify Cleaning Products

To be sincere, I'm a piece of a advertising hater.

Don't get me incorrect, I love a capitalist society wherein cash is the device through which you can assemble empires due to the fact in reality absolutely everyone have a threat at innovating and constructing empires (even though it does suck that a few have it one billion times simpler throughout the scary "getting commenced" years because of the wealth they're born into).

However, I hate the abundance of advertising and marketing and advertising and advertising and marketing we enjoy as corporations attempt to get their products in our arms.

Because of advertising and advertising and advertising and advertising, we're in ordinary anxiety of questions which consist of:

Am I searching for the right element?

Am I looking for enough (consider the laundry detergent hassle?)

Is this product higher than what I'm the use of?

Are there germs in my residence? (and yes, yes there are. Germs are everywhere because of the truth they may be alleged to be there).

Will this product make it more strong for my family at some degree inside the cold and flu season?

Etc

And it is able to deliver us greater anxieties than we realise what to do with.

Don't deliver in!

But Rachel, how do I combat this?